A Friendly Letter to Skeptics and Atheists

MUSINGS ON WHY GOD IS GOOD AND FAITH ISN'T EVIL

David G. Myers

JOSSEY-BASS
A Wiley Imprint
www.josseybass.com

Published by Jossey-Bass
A Wiley Imprint
989 Market Street, San Francisco, CA 94103-1741—www.josseybass.com

Readers should be aware that Internet Web sites offered as citations and/or sources for further information may have changed or disappeared between the time this was written and when it is read.

Jossey-Bass books and products are available through most bookstores. To contact Jossey-Bass directly call our Customer Care Department within the U.S. at 800-956-7739, outside the U.S. at 317-572-3986, or fax 317-572-4002.

Jossey-Bass also publishes its books in a variety of electronic formats. Some content that appears in print may not be available in electronic books.

Library of Congress Cataloging-in-Publication Data

Myers, David G.
    A friendly letter to skeptics and atheists : musings on why God is good and faith isn't evil / David G. Myers.—1st ed.
        p.   cm.
    Includes bibliographical references.
    ISBN 978-0-470-29027-9 (cloth)
        1. Christianity and atheism.   2. Skepticism.   3. Apologetics.   I. Title.
BR128.A8M94 2008
261.2'1—dc22

                                                                                    2008014794

Printed in the United States of America
FIRST EDITION
HB Printing   10 9 8 7 6 5 4 3 2 1

All royalties from the sale of this book are assigned to the David and Carol Myers Foundation, which exists to receive and distribute funds to other charitable organizations.

Contents

Preface

Intellectual history records several rounds of atheist attacks on religion. Arguably, none have been more visible than the early-twenty-first-century "new atheist" contention that religion—all religions—are both false and toxic. Reading these books and articles as a science-loving religious person triggered some thoughts.

More than sympathizers of these books might suppose, many of us Christians concur with their litanies of our failings. Moreover, given the ever-present tendency of religious people to construct false idols and to associate their own ideas with God's, we need to be challenged by the voices of reason.

The faith tradition that has nurtured me shares considerable common ground with the new atheists. It encourages the humility and curiosity that underlies free-spirited science. It assumes the unity of mind and body (rather than Plato's bodily imprisoned immortal soul). And it does not view God as a celestial vending machine controlled by our prayers.

Psychological science, which it is my vocation to report on in textbooks and other writings, offers big ideas that are deeply congenial with big ideas from Jewish-Christian thought. Human nature looks much the same, whether viewed through the lens of ancient biblical wisdom or modern psychological science.

Although religion in some forms has indeed fed prejudice and atrocity, the available evidence is pretty compelling: In the Western world, at least, religiosity is more often associated with good—with happiness, health, generosity, and volunteering—than with evil.

I develop and offer these and other reflections not as a sophisticated defense of theism (I leave it to others to engage the new atheists, whose critical intelligence I respect, on philosophical issues such as the problem of evil). My ambition is also not so bold as the reverse of Richard Dawkins' hope that religious readers will be atheists when they put his book, *The God Delusion*, down. I hope, more simply, to help skeptical readers, many of whom are among my esteemed friends, to appreciate the common ground they share with many people of faith. For those whose thinking has moved from the religious thesis to the skeptical antithesis (or vice versa), I offer some

pointers to a science-respecting Christian synthesis.
I aim to suggest to skeptical friends how someone might
share their commitment to reason, evidence, and, yes,
even skepticism while also embracing a faith that makes
sense of the universe, gives meaning to life, connects
us in supportive communities, mandates altruism, and
offers hope in the face of adversity and death.

April 2008

David G. Myers
Holland, Michigan

(handwritten notes)

1. Commitment to TRUTH.
2. Commit to REASON.
3. Commit to love & respect
4.

The nature of God.
The nature of His revelation
Our understanding

For Malcolm A. Jeeves,
exemplar of scientific rigor and humane faith

science derogate

1. Belief in God is irrational. ← ilogical
   ← hipocr

2. Belief in God is dangerous.
   - jihad / crusades
   - bigotry / sectarianism (Nothn Irlnd) / Isrel - Palistn
   - gay bashing - homophobic

3. Religion is intolerant.

- CLIMATE CHANGE DENIERS
ANTIABORTION , ANTI-GAY MARRIAGE ,

-

God reveals himself through nature / creation.   true
                                                  imge.
∴ if we reject true image & nature we reject God

   - people rejected Jesus in the same way
Jn 5:39 - study scripture diligently yet reject Jn
Mk 12:9 - stone builds yet has become corner sn.

False and Dangerous?

Mindful of the God-professing but war-making American president, the faith-inspired atrocity of 9/11, the gay-bashing (and sometimes gay) ministers and politicians, the religious opposition to medical stem cell research, and the science-denigrating creationists, many of you, my secular friends,

> Truth springs from argument amongst friends.
>
> —ATTRIBUTED TO DAVID HUME

understandably have had it with religion. In today's world, believing in God strikes you as an irrational delusion and a social toxin.

You may not vilify religion with the ferocity of the new atheists, but you welcome their exposing religion's inanities, superstitions, and hypocrisies. You may wince when religion-despiser Richard Dawkins (in *The God Delusion*) calls Mother Teresa "sanctimoniously hypocritical" and mocks Jews who "nod maniacally towards a wall." You may know better than to join

Dawkins in savaging religion by associating it with its worst extremes, such as homophobic nut case Fred Phelps and self-appointed God-channel Pat Robertson. You may even welcome Martin Luther King Jr.'s faith-based justice, Jimmy Carter's faith-based peacemaking, and Barack Obama's faith-based civility.

But with images of yesteryear's crusades and witch hunts and today's suicide bombers and religious tribalisms, you sympathize with Sam Harris' assertion (in *Letter to a Christian Nation*) that religion is "both false and dangerous." You nod when Christopher Hitchens (in *God Is Not Great: How Religion Poisons Everything*) views religion as "violent, irrational, intolerant, allied to racism and tribalism and bigotry, invested in ignorance and hostile to free inquiry, contemptuous of women and coercive toward children."

Mindful of the example of Jesus, a radical critic of the religion of his day, this letter responds, first, by affirming many of your indictments of religion, which has indeed often been associated with idiocy and evil. Throughout history, people have been eager to domesticate God, to fashion and worship golden calves, to justify their own thoughts and actions by identifying them with a supposed divine will. If skeptics identify irrational images of God and nature, so much the better for their skepticism. This letter responds, second, by indicating how many of us "dyed-in-the-wool faith-heads" (to accept Professor Dawkins' aspersion) nevertheless find a progressive, biblically rooted, "ever-reforming" faith to be reasonable, meaningful, hopeful, inspiring, science-affirming, and profoundly humane.

My Assumptions

As a Christian monotheist and a psychological scientist, I approach life and work with two unoriginal assumptions: that (1) there is a God and (2) it's not me (and it's also not you). Together these axioms imply my surest conviction: some of my beliefs (like yours) contain error. We are finite and fallible. We have dignity but not deity.

This biblical understanding is why I further believe that we should hold our own untested beliefs tentatively, assess others' ideas with open-minded skepticism, and when appropriate, use observation and experimentation to winnow error from truth.

This ideal of faith-supported humility and skepticism, arising from a religious tradition that calls itself "reformed and ever-reforming," has helped motivate my own research and science writing. Truth cannot be found merely by searching our own small minds; there is not enough there. So we put our ideas to the test. If they survive, so much the better for them.

If they crash against a wall of evidence, it is time to rethink. "All truth is God's truth," we're fond of saying. So let the chips fall as they may.

Within psychological science, this ever-reforming process has many times changed my mind, leading me now to believe that newborns are not the blank slates I once presumed, that electroconvulsive therapy often alleviates intractable depression, that America's economic growth has not improved our morale, that the automatic unconscious mind dwarfs the conscious mind, that personality is unrelated to birth order, that traumatic experiences rarely get repressed, that most folks have positive self-esteem (which sometimes causes problems), and that sexual orientation is not a choice.

Not all questions are amenable to science. Leo Tolstoy's short list of ultimate questions—"Why should I live?" "Why should I do anything?" "Is there in life any purpose which the inevitable death that awaits me does not undo and destroy?"—are beyond the bounds of my psychological science. But science can shed light on most of today's culture war issues. If we think capital punishment does (or does not) deter crime more than other available punishments, we can utter our personal opinion. Or we can ask whether states with a death penalty have lower homicide rates, whether their rates have dropped after instituting the death penalty, and whether they have risen when abandoning the death penalty.

In checking our personal opinions against reality, we emulate the empiricism of Moses: "If a prophet speaks in the name of the Lord and what he says does not come true, then it is not the Lord's message." The same empirical spirit was exemplified in the New Testament by the wise Gamaliel when religious leaders wanted to kill the apostle Peter and his compatriots for refusing to submit to their authority. Leave them alone, counseled Gamaliel, "because if this plan or this undertaking is of human origin, it will fail; but if it is of God, you will not be able to overthrow them." As Paul advised the Thessalonians, "Test everything; hold fast to what is good."

So for the most part, my skeptical friends, I share your skepticism. As an appreciative longtime subscriber to *The Skeptical Inquirer* and to Michael Shermer's interesting *Skeptic's Society* mailings, I cheer on challenges to rampant irrationalism. Thus my *Psychology* (8th edition) begins with a chapter on "thinking critically with psychological science" and thereafter offers scientific analyses of alternative medicine, astrology, ESP, near-death experiences, repression, hypnosis, and lots more. I have critically examined the supposed powers of unchecked intuition (in *Intuition: Its Powers and Perils*). And I enjoy casting a critical eye on intriguing claims by asking "What do you mean?" and "How do you know?"

Framed positively, the new atheist books are not just an attack on mindless, unbending religion but an affirmation of reason, evidence, and critical intelligence. Therein lies our common ground. We *agree*: let's, with a spirit of humility, put testable ideas to the test and then let's throw out religion's dirty bathwater. And we *differ*: is there amid the bathwater a respect-worthy baby—a reasonable and beneficial faith?

Mea Culpa

You, my skeptical friends, understandably accuse
us faith-heads of hypocrisy. Of preaching love and
practicing lust. Of teaching compassion for "all God's
children" and displaying indifference or bigotry. Of
proclaiming allegiance to truth while turning a blind eye
to evidence. Of wedding great political power with great
stupidity. Of wielding a few biblical "clobber passages"
against women and gays. Of advocating humility and
actualizing self-righteousness.

More readily than you might suppose, many of us
agree. Across mainline Christendom (the faith tradition
from and for which I speak, leaving others to speak for
theirs), we, as part of our weekly rhythm of worship,
confess our falling short of our ideals of love and charity.
In the historical Latin Mass, worshipers confess their
flaws and failures:

peccavi nimis cogitatione, verbo et opere:
mea culpa,

---

mea culpa,

mea maxima culpa.

I have sinned exceedingly,

in thought, word and deed:

through my fault,

through my fault,

through my most grievous fault.

Most Protestant worship similarly confesses and seeks forgiveness for sins. "Forgive us our trespasses/debts/sins" lies at the heart of Christendom's oft-voiced Lord's Prayer. We have sinned in what we have done and in what we have left undone, in what we have said and in what we have left unsaid. We are "miserable offenders," acknowledges the historic Anglican Book of Common Prayer.

You accuse us of hypocrisy, stupidity, pride, and a failure to love? Well, we accuse ourselves of as much and more. Even Pope Benedict XVI admitted, "There exist pathologies in religion that are extremely dangerous and that make it necessary to see the divine light of reason as a 'controlling organ.'" Today's Protestant prophets remind their own churches never to be in the pocket of any political party. Authentic biblical religion calls its followers to "do justice" and to be stewards of God's creation. If we have abetted poverty, injustice, climate change, genocide, or unjust war, then *shame on us*.

If we have fostered superstition or tolerated prejudice (as we have), show us our error. Have our elected national leaders (self-described Christians, no less) acted 180 degrees in opposition to the Old Testament admonition to give our hungry enemies "bread to eat"? to Saint Paul's instruction to "overcome evil with good"? Have we neglected Jesus' mandates to "turn the other cheek" and to "love your enemies and pray for those who persecute you"? If so, the problem lies not with the religious wisdom but with us, its human vehicles. The dynamics of in-group versus out-group, of corrupting power, of egotism and evil, operate within religion and without. *Mea culpa.*

> If we let human beings into our religion, it is going to get corrupted.
>
> —KEITH WARD, *IS RELIGION DANGEROUS?* (2007)

The Dance of Fanatics and Infidels

The new atheism tells us to take our pick: science or theism, reason or faith. Only one can win. Get on the science train—accept its evolutionary understanding—and inevitably, Richard Dawkins believes, you will find yourself arriving at the destination called atheism. Indeed, he not only

> The greatest empiricists among us . . . when left to their instincts . . . dogmatize like infallible Popes.
>
> —WILLIAM JAMES, THE WILL TO BELIEVE (1897)

disagrees with religious ideas—"I am attacking God, all gods, anything and everything supernatural"—he even disagrees with tolerating religious ideas and enabling their viruslike spread. "What is really pernicious is the practice of teaching children that faith itself is a virtue. Faith is an evil precisely because it requires no justification and brooks no argument. . . . Faith can be very, very dangerous, and deliberately to implant it into the vulnerable mind of an innocent child is a grievous wrong."

When voiced by scientists, dogmatic atheism makes life more difficult for mainstream science supporters such as Alan Leshner, director of the American Association for the Advancement of Science. His first rule of "science and public engagement" is this: "*Never pit science against religion.*" Michael Ruse, a self-described agnostic and "hard-line Darwinian," argued in a widely distributed e-mail to the philosopher-skeptic Daniel Dennett that Dennett and Dawkins were "absolute disasters in the fight against intelligent design. . . . We are in a fight, and we need to make allies in the fight, not simply alienate everyone of good will."

Could we agree, my skeptical friends, that Professor Dawkins and his kindred spirits confirm fundamentalists' long-held fear: that teaching evolution leads to atheism? Fundamentalists always said "that Darwinism equals atheism," notes Ruse, "and now the Darwinians apparently agree!" Phillip Johnson credits Dawkins' evolutionary atheism for inspiring intelligent design theory. (Johnson's challenge to evolutionary theory, the great organizing principle of biology, began after he picked up Dawkins' *Blind Watchmaker* in a London bookstore and engaged its contentions that life is a mere manifestation of blind physics and that religion is a virus.)

Secularists understandably react in opposition to fundamentalist zealotry and scientific ignorance.

And religious fundamentalists understandably react when told they are, in so many words, "deranged, deluded, deceived and deceiving." In Henrik Ibsen's play *The Wild Duck*, the dispiriting Gregers Werle was bent on demolishing people's illusions. Better to face the facts, he assumed, than to live a life based on a lie. The new atheists agree, in seeing a world with, as Dawkins says, "no design, no purpose, no evil and good, nothing but blind pitiless indifference." And if the universe is meaningless, they say, we might as well get over thinking it otherwise.

Given that message, should it surprise us that many people have responded by tuning out science and welcoming conservative fundamentalisms? "Fanatics and infidels have their ways of keeping each other in business," observes the anthropologist Richard Schweder.

Simplistic Stereotypes

Consider a well-established phenomenon: people readily recognize the diversity within their own groups while often overestimating the uniformity of other groups. The phenomenon is known to social psychologists by various names, including "out-group homogeneity bias." In everyday language, it is "we differ; they are alike." To people of one race, those of another even seem to look more alike.

Perhaps you've noticed that people on the outside overgeneralize about the groups you are part of. They just don't understand how varied are the people who live where you do, work where you do, worship or recreate where you do, or look like you do. But as a member of such communities, you understand how diverse you all are.

Thus believers may have caricaturized images of the prototypical atheist (perhaps lumping Stalin with today's humane scientific secularists). And to judge from their recent books, atheists sometimes return the favor by equating religion with its irrational aberrations. Richard Dawkins and Sam Harris itemize seeming religious lunacies, including the nasty practices listed in Leviticus, as if they had the same standing as the later teachings of the second author of Isaiah or of Jesus' beatitudes (for example, "Blessed are the peacemakers"). "This is like talking of chemistry in terms of phlogiston and bodily humours, and mocking it for its crudity," observes the theologian Keith Ward, once a colleague of Dawkins' at Oxford.

To lump together Mennonites, Reform Jews, and the Taliban—labeling them all as "religion" (as when Sam Harris writes that "All religions [are] dangerous" or Dawkins says that "faith is one of the world's great evils")—is to gloss over some very important distinctions. Catholic liberation theology

> Rather than treating religions, as so many enlightened people do, as a relic of the past, long on passion and short on reason, the West will best learn to differentiate between moderate civil religious interpretations and violence-prone fundamentalist ones.
>
> —AMITAI ETZIONI, "THE WEST NEEDS A SPIRITUAL SURGE" (2007)

and jihadist beheadings are, um, a little different. Fellow evolutionist (and self-described atheist) David Sloan Wilson reminds Dawkins that "religions are *diverse*, in the same way that species in ecosystems are diverse. Rather than issuing monolithic statements about religion, evolutionists need to explain religious diversity in the same way that they explain biological diversity." To paraphrase the *Sesame Street* jingle, "Some of these things are not like the others."

So please, skeptical friends, resist the out-group homogeneity bias. Don't lump all faith-heads together.

The Heart of Science and Religion

You skeptics remind me, and rightly so, of the church's
opposition to scientific advances—of its condemnation
of Galileo's heliocentrism and Darwin's evolutionism
and of its onetime supernatural explanations of various
natural phenomena: disease, earthquakes, storms, and
even human behavior. Nevertheless, between purposeless
naturalism and antiscience fundamentalism lies a third
alternative: a faith-rooted rationality that helped give
birth to science.

Many science historians contend, as Harvard
astronomer and science historian Owen Gingerich
has said, that "the Judeo-Christian philosophical
framework has proved to be a particularly fertile
ground for the rise of modern science." The science-
fostering theology went something like this: if, as once
supposed, nature is sacred—if nature is animated with
river goddesses and sun gods—then we ought not
tamper with it. However, if nature is not God but God's
orderly and intelligible creation, then let us, as rational

creatures made in God's image, explore this handiwork
and discover the divine laws. We glimpse this idea
in both the Psalms ("The firmament proclaims his
handiwork") and Saint Paul ("Ever since the creation
of the world his eternal power and divine nature,
invisible though they are, have been understood and
seen through the things he has made").

So let us observe and experiment, believing
that whatever God found worth creating, we should
find worth studying. Moreover, let us do so freely,
knowing that our ultimate allegiance is not to any
human authority or human doctrine but to God alone.
As the seventeenth-century geographer Nathanael
Carpenter wrote, "I am free. I am bound to nobody's
word, except to those inspired by God; if I oppose
these in the least degree, I beseech God to forgive me
my audacity of judgment, as I have been moved not so
much by longing for some opinion of my own as by
love for the freedom of science." Science, by putting
competing ideas to the test, helps restrain unchecked
illusory thinking among people who are tempted, in
the words of Saint Paul, to "turn away from listening
to the truth, and wander away to myths."

Historically, this Christian view of God and nature
helped motivate the pioneering scientific thinking of
Francis Bacon, Galileo Galilei, Johannes Kepler, Blaise
Pascal, and Isaac Newton. Mendel's genetics were

the work of an Augustinian monk. For Copernicus, a cathedral canon, astronomy was a divine science. These scientific Magellans believed that "God

> The laws of nature are written in a sort of cosmic code, [and the scientist's job] is to crack the code and reveal the message—nature's message, God's message, take your choice.
>
> —PAUL DAVIES, "GLIMPSING THE MIND OF GOD" (2006)

did it." But rather than let that potential conversation stopper shut off their curiosity, they wondered how God did it. They thought that by figuring that out, they might glimpse the mind of God. God created the world with an intelligent plan, which was discernible through reason and science; the world—nature—revealed not only useful knowledge but also God's wisdom and beauty.

Moreover, their aim was to submit their human ideas to the test, knowing that if nature did not conform to them, then so much the worse for their ideas. If scientists' data indicated that the earth was not stationary, they must abandon the presumption that heavenly bodies circled the earth. Reason, they believed, must be aided by observation and experimentation in matters of science and by spiritual insight in matters of faith. Whether searching for truth in the book of God's word or the book of God's works, they viewed themselves in God's service. They were scientists not despite their faith but partly *because* of their faith. Doing good science was less a right than a religious duty.

And so it is for their intellectual descendants today. Christendom gave birth not only to famous settings that have nourished so much scholarship and science—Oxford, Cambridge, Harvard, Princeton, and the like—but also to countless other grassroots wellsprings of science. I am writing this book from my office in a $37 million science building at a place called Hope, a faith-based liberal arts college with Calvinist roots, whose signature departments are in the natural sciences. In one recent summer, 171 students were working around me in full-time research, supported by faculty research grants and by National Science Foundation summer grants to six science departments (more than at any other liberal arts college). Nearly one in four students graduates with a science or engineering degree, and hundreds have earned science Ph.D.'s. One former student, a Nobel laureate for pioneering nanotechnology, reflected on Hope College's lingering influence on his work, which "is based on the faith that when God made the universe, he wired into the laws of physics and chemistry a path. . . . All I have to do is go find that path that God put there in the beginning." My point is not that students are thinking God when walking into a computational biology lab but simply that the image of religion-friendly places' being unfriendly to science is not the reality I live with.

Indeed, the scientist's religious mandate, wrote the neuroscientist Donald MacKay, "is to 'tell it like it is,' knowing that the Author is at our elbow, a silent judge of the accuracy with which we claim to describe the world He has created." Disciplined, rigorous inquiry—checking our theories against reality—helps fulfill Jesus' "great commandment" to love God not just with our hearts but also with our minds. As Jesus intimated, we have much to learn: "I still have many things to say to you, but you cannot bear them now. When the Spirit of the truth comes, he will guide you into all the truth."

The Skeptics' Boys Club

Much as I love empiricism and cold-blooded rationality, I must acknowledge a reality that perhaps you have noticed too: all the hard-nosed skeptics I have so far mentioned, as well as most of their kindred spirits, have one thing in common. They are white males. Ditto the ten winners and fourteen runners-up on the *Skeptical Inquirer* list of outstanding twentieth-century rationalist skeptics—all men. In the "science and the paranormal" section of the 2007 Prometheus Books catalogue, from the leading publisher of skeptical books, one can find ninety-four male and four female authors. In one Skeptics Society survey, nearly four in five respondents were men. Likewise, when I attended a jammed 2006 Skeptics Society lecture by Sam Harris at Cal Tech, I discovered that the audience was overwhelmingly guys like me.

By comparison, 52 percent of the authors of books that I know to acclaim intuition's powers are female. And of the 253 books in the New Age section at our local Barnes and Noble superstore, 37 percent were female.

I wondered, does the oft-reported gender
difference in openness to nonrational ways of knowing
carry over to participation in faith communities?
Analyzing data from more than forty-six thousand
people responding to National Opinion Research Center
surveys since 1972, I found that 23 percent of men
and 33 percent of women reported attending religious
services weekly or more. And 43 percent of men and
66 of women have reported praying daily or more. Men
are also three times as likely as women to say they never
pray and, depending on the survey, are two to three
times more likely to declare themselves atheists ("don't
believe in God"). Likewise, blacks more than whites
have reported frequently attending church and praying.
(One in four whites, but only one in ten blacks, reports
praying less than once a week.)

The maleness and paleness of skepticism doesn't
clue us to who's correct. But could we agree that they
reveal an interesting cultural phenomenon: aggressive
antireligious skepticism is predominantly a product of
Euro-American white men, who often are expressing
contempt for the beliefs of people quite different from
themselves.

Readers who cherish cold rationalism, as I do
to a great extent, will cheer the skeptic guys on. Let
reason rule! But we might also pause to consider new
research on multiple forms of human intelligence and

especially on the importance of emotion for human cognition. We humans are a uniquely emotional species, capable of emotional intelligence, empathy, and emotion-informed thinking. Adaptive human intelligence is more than cold reason.

The neuroscientist Antonio Damasio illustrates this point with the case of one man who lost his ability to experience emotion after surgery for a brain tumor. Although his rational intelligence remained intact (he could think but not feel), his social judgments became dysfunctional, and he lost both his job and his marriage. Other patients, having lost their memories of emotions related to their experiences of success and failure, erred more when assessing risks in a laboratory gambling task. On this task, most people make money, as the emotions generated by their unconscious brain figure things out ahead of their conscious reasoning. Without these feelings to inform their thinking, the emotionless patients typically lost money.

This illustrates a big lesson from today's psychological science: pure reason is half-witted. Emotion and reason, like warp and woof, together weave the fabric of our minds. As Blaise Pascal foresaw, "The heart has its reasons."

Faith, too, is an expression not only of the mind but also of the heart. So it was for the legendary science writer Martin Gardner, who, after a lifetime of brilliant

A FRIENDLY LETTER TO SKEPTICS AND ATHEISTS

Ls Jesus did - he ate ū sinners & the religios.
Paul du - he spoke @ the areopolosis

debunking of pseudoscience and things paranormal,
explained why he was not an atheist. After defending the
reasonableness of letting the heart take over when the
head cannot decide, he concluded that "I have no basis
whatever for my belief in God other than a passionate
longing that God exist and that I and others will not
cease to exist. Because I believe with my heart that God
upholds all things, it follows that I believe my leap
of faith, in a way beyond my comprehension, is God
outside of me asking and wanting me to believe, and
God within me responding."

That said, reason and evidence *should* rule on ideas
that science can put to the test. So are we scientists of
faith indeed open to evidence that challenges popular
religious presumptions? Are we, skeptics wonder, open
to data that dispute cherished beliefs? It's a fair question.
Before noting some ways in which science affirms
religious wisdom, let's acknowledge its challenges
to three specific presumptions of popular religion:
the existence of an immortal soul, the potency of
petitionary prayers, and the plausibility of a created
universe.

Is God
Testing us ?

Does he expect
us to ignore logic /...

What does God use
Cm us -   FAITH
         THEN

FAITH . Sure d what we
       hope for, calid whe we do M...

- True y Reasonable   (AC)
God is a god of order not cha (?)
God hates lies   (?)
Not test us beyond what we ca bear
- Abraham reasoned God would
     give him Isacc bcd reli, C... h

Inseparable Body and Soul

Today's behavior genetics and neuroscience teach
a compelling and provocative lesson: everything
psychological is also biological. Our every idea,
every mood, every urge is a biological happening.
We love, laugh, and cry with our bodies. Without our
bodies—including our brains and our ancestral history
represented in our genes—we are nobodies. To think,
feel, or act without a body would be like running
without legs. In the scientific view, our human essence
cannot be conceived as disembodied.

Today's cognitive neuroscience specifies brain-
mind connections. In monkeys, neuropsychologists
have detected specific cells that buzz with activity
in response to a specific face or to a specific type of
perceived body movement. In humans, detectable brain
activity coincides with, and even slightly precedes,
the instant at which a person consciously decides to
perform an action, such as lifting a finger. Moreover,
we are learning how abnormalities in the brain's

chemical messengers—its neurotransmitters—underlie psychological disorders such as depression and schizophrenia. Each such advance further tightens the links between brain and mind.

And those insights are having a profound effect on the way we see ourselves and the world. Indeed, it becomes more and more difficult to see human nature as composed of two entities: material body and immaterial essence or mind or soul. In the seventeenth century, it could seem to the dualist Descartes that "I am . . . lodged in my body as a pilot in a vessel." To the scientifically informed twenty-first-century person, to whom consciousness is the vapors of brain activity, this seems an illusory intuition.

That is not to say that the mind's *significance* is reducible to nothing but brain. It's people—mind-brain packages—who speak, think, and feel. If we describe the EXIT sign over an emergency door only in terms of circuits and lights, we fail to account for its message. If we reduce the mind to the brain, we lose something important: the mind. In *The End of Faith*, even the atheist Sam Harris appreciates a spirituality that wonders at the mystery of matter giving rise to conscious mind.

Yet the mind is not an extra entity that occupies the brain. As the Nobel laureate psychologist Roger Sperry emphasized, "Everything in science to date seems to indicate that conscious awareness is a property of the living brain and inseparable from it." We are not ghosts (or souls) in machines but unified mind-brain systems.

Longing for a nonmaterial spiritual dimension, some people look to out-of-body extrasensory perception—to reports of people predicting the future, reading others' minds, or discerning events at remote locations. Alas, no greedy—or charitable—psychic has been able to predict the outcome of a lottery jackpot or to make billions on the stock market. The search for a valid and reliable test of ESP has resulted in thousands of experiments. The closest we have come was a controlled procedure that invited "senders" to transmit telepathically one of four visual images to "receivers" deprived of sensation in a nearby chamber. The result? A reported 32 percent accurate response rate, surpassing the chance rate of 25 percent. But follow-up studies have consistently failed to replicate the supposed phenomenon.

One skeptic, the magician James Randi, has a long-standing offer—now $1 million—"to anyone who proves a genuine psychic power under proper observing conditions." French, Australian, and Indian groups have parallel offers of up to 200,000 Euro to anyone with demonstrable paranormal abilities. And $50 million was available for information leading to Osama bin Ladin's capture. Large as these sums are, the scientific seal of approval would be worth far more to anyone whose supernatural powers could be authenticated.

To refute those who say there is no ESP, one need only produce a single person who can demonstrate a single, reproducible ESP phenomenon. (To refute those who say pigs can't talk would take but one talking pig.) So far, no such person has emerged. Randi's offer has been publicized for three decades, and dozens of people have been tested, sometimes under the scrutiny of an independent panel of judges. Still, nothing. No evidence of a human mind or essence that operates independently of the body.

Nor has science been friendly to mystical interpretations of those near-death experiences that are recalled by about one-third of people who have brushed death through a trauma such as cardiac arrest. To the psychiatric researcher Ronald Siegel, the typical near-death experience does not indicate a mind or soul leaping free of the body. Rather, its replay of old memories, out-of-body sensations, and visions of tunnels or funnels and bright light strikingly resembles the typical hallucinogenic experience. Temporal lobe seizures, sensory deprivation, and oxygen deprivation can produce similar visions. Perhaps, surmises Siegel, the bored or stressed or oxygen-deprived brain manufactures the near-death experience as a "hallucinatory activity of the brain." It's like gazing out a window as dusk encroaches. We begin to see the reflected interior of the room as if it were outside.

The emerging scientific view that we are unified mind-brain systems does, then, challenge the oft-presumed religious idea that we are made of two realities, body and soul. Actually, say a broad swath of today's biblical scholars and theologians, that's a Platonic, not a biblical, idea. "Does not death mean that the body comes to exist by itself, separated from the soul?" asks Socrates in Plato's *Phaedo*. For Socrates, drinking the hemlock was the soul's liberation. It was fundamentally *not* dying.

This is quite unlike the implicit psychology of the Old Testament people, whose *nephesh* (soul) terminates at death. In the Hebrew view, we do not *have* a *nephesh*; we *are* *nephesh* (living beings). In most of its eight hundred Old Testament occurrences, biblical scholars report, this *nephesh* is akin to the soul we have in mind when saying "there wasn't a soul (person) in the room" or "I love you from the depths of my soul" (being).

The New Testament similarly offers us whole persons—"souls" who can eat and drink. Death is not liberation of the soul, not mere "passing away," but in Saint Paul's words "the great enemy." We are dust to dust, ashes to ashes. The Easter hope of life after death is not something intrinsic to our nature—something that

Does it distinguish conscious beings from non-sentient?

Jesus resurrected was able to eat & drink!

30

is our birthright with or without God—but rather God-given. Thus Christendom's Apostle's Creed proclaims not the immortality of

> It is easier, perhaps, to hope for or even believe in an afterlife without faith in a personal God. One simply regards survival as part of the nature of things.
>
> —MARTIN GARDNER, "FAITH: WHY I AM NOT AN ATHEIST" (1999)

the soul but the renewal through the Resurrection of some sort of bodily existence, the only conceivable existence in the biblical view.

Ahem, the skeptics say. The idea that real death (as Jesus experienced on Good Friday) will be transformed (as on his Resurrection at Easter) is no less fantastic a claim than that of an undying human essence. Agreed, this is the ultimate audacity of hope. But grant this much: unlike Platonic dualism, which did influence the church's past theology, this biblical understanding is fundamentally congenial with the scientific understanding of human nature. Both agree that our minds are nothing apart from our bodies. We are, now and in eternity (the Christian hopes), bodies alive. Both the scientific and biblical worldviews assume—in contradiction to spiritualist claims of reincarnation, astral projection, and seances with the dead—that without our bodies we are nothing. As C. S. Lewis once wrote, "If the Psychical Researchers succeeded in

should Samuel?

31

proving 'survival' . . . they would not be supporting the Christian faith but refuting it."

If indeed we are embodied minds and mindful bodies, then we should care about ourselves and others, living bodies and all. (No wonder Christians have been so active in spreading hospitals and medicine.) Our spirituality is rooted not in possessing a thing but in deep feelings of connection and devotion to something much larger than self.

Does Prayer "Work"?

If you are a secular skeptic, you likely also roll your eyes at televangelists praying for healing, for safety, for success, for rain or an end to rain. You have heard people of faith share their experiences of answered prayers for a child's safe return home, for guidance on a business venture, even for a parking place. For many of us psychologists, hearing such stories brings to mind experiments that show how readily we perceive relationships where none exist (especially where we expect to see them), think that one thing causes another when they really are only coincidentally correlated, and believe that we are controlling events that are actually beyond our control.

These experiments have been extended to studies of gambling behavior, stock market predictions, superstitious behavior, and intuitions about ESP. The unchallenged verdict: we easily misperceive our behavior as correlated with subsequent events, and thus we easily delude ourselves into thinking that we can predict or control uncontrollable events.

*If we easily connect things th ore rndo.
hou do we kno pryes ore asooed?*

So, you understandably ask, might illusory thinking contaminate people's beliefs regarding the power of their petitionary and intercessory prayers? If we are predisposed to find order in random events, to interpret outcomes guided by our preconceptions, and to search for and recall instances that confirm our beliefs, then might we overestimate the efficacy of petitionary prayer? Is prayer not a made-to-order arena for illusory thinking?

If that sounds heretical, it may reassure fellow faith-heads to remember that warnings about false prayer come from believers as well as skeptics. There was no stronger skeptic of false piety than Jesus: "When you are praying, do not heap up empty phrases . . . for your Father knows what you need before you ask him." If it is heretical to think too little of the power of our prayers, it is more heretical to think of God as a celestial Santa Claus.

Well, then, say some researchers from both the skeptic and believer camps, why not settle the issue empirically? Why not put prayer to the test? So they did.

Modern prayer experiments bring to fruition the "prayer test challenge" envisioned in 1872 by an anonymous Briton. In that challenge, one single ward or hospital would be chosen to receive three to five years of sustained prayer by "the whole body of the faithful." Would its patients' healing and mortality rates surpass those in comparable hospitals elsewhere?

34

The proposal triggered a national "prayer-gauge controversy" that raged for a year. For many people, the very idea of testing prayer—and God—was outrageous. If experimenting with prayer offends, said the Victorian polymath Francis Galton, then why not examine the efficacy of spontaneous prayers? Galton collected mortality data on people who were the subjects of much prayer, such as kings, and reported that they did not outlive others. Moreover, the proportion of stillbirths suffered by praying and nonpraying expectant parents appeared similar.

And there things stood quietly for a century, until American researchers decided they would experiment with prayer. Randolph Byrd's 1988 report, titled "Positive Therapeutic Effects of Intercessory Prayer in a Coronary Care Unit Population," helped reignite both scientific and popular interest in prayer. Byrd randomly assigned 393 coronary patients either to a no-prayer group or to a group that would receive prayer from three to seven "born again" intercessors. For six of twenty-six outcomes, the prayed-for patients did better. Although there were questions about whether the person recording the data was entirely ignorant of the patient assignment, the widely publicized conclusion was that prayer worked. For the other measures—such as length of hospital stay and even mortality—there was, however, no difference between the prayer and no-prayer groups.

The ambiguous results helped inspire Herbert Benson, a Harvard Medical School professor and director of the Mind-Body Institute, to propose in 1997 a substantial and elegantly simple study of the "therapeutic effects of intercessory prayer." With funding from the science-friendly John Templeton Foundation, more than eighteen hundred consenting coronary bypass patients were to be assigned to one of three groups: one that knew that it was being prayed for by volunteer intercessors, one that did not know whether it was being prayed for (but was), and a third group that did not know whether it was being prayed for (and wasn't).

As a Templeton Foundation adviser, I got wind of the experiment and had an opportunity to join several others in questioning our respected fellow Templeton adviser, Herbert Benson, about his proposal and also to question the foundation's wisdom in investing in this project. To me, the idea of testing prayer seemed (based on both my theology and the science of illusory thinking) destined to produce a null result. So I filed a notarized statement suggesting "why people of faith can expect null effects in the Harvard Prayer Experiment." I put this on record in 1997 so that my understanding of authentic Christian prayer would not later seem, if offered after the published results, like after-the-fact rationalization. I also wrote articles and a book chapter expressing my Christian and scientific skepticism about the prayer experiments. Much as C. S. Lewis suggested that evidence of immortality would do more to refute Christianity than support it, so I suggested three reasons why "my understanding of God and God's relation to the created world would be more challenged by positive than negative results":

1. The prayer concept being tested is more akin to magic than to a biblical understanding of prayer to an omniscient and sovereign God. In the biblical view, God underlies all of creation. God is not some little spiritual factor that

> [Prayer] is not an attempt to force God's hand, but a humble acknowledgment of helplessness and dependence.
>
> —J. I. PACKER, EVANGELISM AND THE SOVEREIGNTY OF GOD (1961)

occasionally deflects nature's course but is rather the ground of all being. God works not in the gaps of what we don't yet understand but in and through nature, including the healing ministries that led people of faith to spread medicine and hospitals worldwide. Thus while our Lord's model prayer encourages us to acknowledge our dependence on God for our basic necessities ("our daily bread"), it does not view God as a celestial vending machine whose levers we pull with our prayers. Indeed, would the all-wise, all-knowing, all-loving God of the Bible be uninformed or uncaring were it not for our prayers? Does presuming that we creatures can pull God's strings not violate biblical admonitions to humbly recognize our place as finite creatures of the infinite God? No wonder we are counseled to offer prayers of adoration, praise, confession, thanksgiving, dedication, and meditation, as well as to ask for what shall (spiritually, if not materially) be given.

2. Even for those who believe that God intervenes in response to our prayers, there are practical reasons for expecting null effects:

- The "noise" factor: Given that 95 percent of Americans express belief in God, all patients undergoing cardiac bypass surgery will already be receiving prayer—by spouses, children, siblings, friends, colleagues, and fellow believers, and congregants—if not offering them themselves. Are these fervent prayers a mere "noise factor" above which the signal of additional prayers may rouse God? Does God follow a dose-response curve—more prayers, more response? Does God count votes? Are the pleading, earnest prayers of patients and those who love them not sufficiently persuasive (if God needs to be informed or persuaded of our needs)? Are the distant prayers of strangers participating in an experiment additionally needed?

- *The doubt factor.* To be sure, some Christians believe that prayers, uttered in believing faith, are potent. But are there any or many people of faith who also believe that prayers called forth by a doubting (open-minded, testing) scientist will be similarly effective?

- *"God is not mocked."* As Christians recalled during the 1872 British prayer test controversy, Jesus declared in response to one of his temptations that we ought not put "God to the test." Reflecting on a proposal to test prayers for randomly selected preterm babies, Keith Stewart Thompson questions "whether all such experiments come close to blasphemy. If the health outcomes of the prayed-for subjects turn out to be significantly better than for the others, the experimenter will have set up a situation in which God has, as it were, been made to show his (or her) hand." C. S. Lewis observed, regarding any effort to prove prayer, that the "impossibility of empirical proof is a spiritual necessity" lest a person begin to "feel like a magician." Indeed, if this experiment were to show that numbers of people praying matter—that distant strangers' prayers boost recovery chances—might rich people not want, in hopes of gaining God's attention, to pay others to pray for them?

3. The evidence of history suggests that *the prayers of finite humans do not manipulate an infinite God.* If they could and did, how many droughts, floods, hurricanes, and plagues would have been averted? How many stillborn infants or children with disabilities would have been born healthy? And consider the Bible's own evidence: How should the unanswered prayers of Job, Paul, and even Jesus inform our theology of prayer? If the rain falls on my picnic, does it mean I pray with too little faith—or that the rain falls on both those who believe and those who don't? Should we pray to God as manipulative adolescents—or as dependent preschoolers, whose loving parents, already knowing their children's needs, welcome the intimacy?

In the ensuing nine years after I offered these thoughts, as we awaited the results from the mother of all prayer experiments, other prayer experiments surfaced:

- A 1997 experiment on "intercessory prayer in the treatment of alcohol abuse and dependence" found no measurable effect of intercessory prayer.

- A 1998 experiment with arthritis patients found no significant effect from distant prayer.

- A 1999 study of 990 coronary care patients— who were unaware of the study—reported about

10 percent fewer complications for the half who received prayers "for a speedy recovery with no complications." But there was no difference in specific major complications such as cardiac arrest, hypertension, and pneumonia. The median hospital stay was the same 4.0 days for both groups.

- A 2001 Mayo Clinic study of 799 coronary care patients offered a simple result: "As delivered in this study, intercessory prayer had no significant effect on medical outcomes."

- A 2005 Duke University study of 848 coronary patients found no significant difference in clinical outcomes between those prayed for and those not.

Amid these negative results, one stunning result temporarily challenged my faith-based skepticism. "Prayer works," said a headline in the *New York Times Magazine* after a 2001 *Journal of Reproductive Medicine* article reported that prayed-for women undergoing in vitro fertilization experienced a 50 percent pregnancy rate—double the 26 percent rate among those not receiving experimental intercessory prayers. As suspicions about the study emerged, one of the study's authors pleaded guilty to criminal business fraud and was sentenced to prison. The article's Columbia University lead author removed his name from the "study," with which it turned out he had no direct involvement. And its other coauthor was discovered to have committed academic fraud (plagiarism) on a prior paper.

Climaxing this string of negative or discredited results came the likely coup de grâce for intercessory prayer experiments: intercessory prayer in the Harvard prayer experiment had no positive effect on recovery from bypass surgery.

If these had been clinical tests of a new drug, the pharmaceutical industry would surely, at this point, say "enough." But imagine that these experiments had confirmed intercessory prayer's clinical efficacy. How big would the "God effect"—if that is how we would have viewed it—need to have been to be added to the list of recommended medical treatments? Or do we err in searching for a "God effect" that is a slight subtraction to, for example, the number of stillbirths or coronary deaths? In the historical Christian understanding, God is not a distant genie whom we call forth with our prayers but rather the creator and sustainer of all that is. Thus when the Pharisees pressed Jesus for some criteria by which they could validate the kingdom of God, Jesus answered, "The kingdom of God is not coming with things that can be observed. . . . For, in fact, the kingdom of God is among you."

The Lord's Prayer, the model prayer for Christians that I pray daily, does not attempt to control a God who withholds care unless cajoled. Rather, by affirming God's nature and our human dependence even for daily bread, it prepares us to receive what God is already providing. One can approach God as a small child might talk with a benevolent parent who knows the child's needs but also cherishes the relationship. Through prayer, people of faith express their praise and gratitude, confess their wrongdoing, voice their heart's concerns and desires, open themselves to the Spirit, and seek the peace and grace to live as God's own people. *Ora et labora*, says the Benedictine motto: pray and work.

The Benevolent, Fine-Tuned Universe

So far I have demonstrated a view of science—and the study of religious topics like prayer—that might not be all that incompatible with your own perspectives as a secular skeptic. Well and good, you say, but what about that great issue at the heart of today's science and religion strife: evolution?

Four hundred years ago, Galileo Galilei made astronomical observations that could make sense only if, contrary to the church's teaching at that time, the earth revolved around the sun. Looking back, we all can appreciate how the church misinterpreted a few poetic biblical verses as scientific teaching ("The sun rises and the sun sets, and hurries back to where it rises"). In censoring Galileo, the church had succumbed to a misinformed vehemence that was foreseen in Proverbs (19:2): "It is not good to have zeal without knowledge."

In the twenty-first century, scientific observation is again clashing with religious zeal. Some 95 percent of scientists polled by Gallup in 1996 agreed that "human beings have developed over millions of years." As a joke with a purpose, the National Center for Science Education invited scientists named "Steve" (in honor of Stephen Jay Gould) to sign their agreement that "evolution is a vital, well-supported, unifying principle of the biological sciences." By late 2007, a total of 854 Steves, mostly biologists, had signed on. Indeed, the evidence has become so compelling that today virtually all biological researchers are convinced that mutation and natural selection explain the emergence and relatedness of all life, including its ingenious designs. "The idea that human minds are the product of evolution is not atheistic theology," declared a 2007 *Nature* editorial. "It is unassailable fact."

Even Darwin would today be astonished at the convergence of evidence supporting his big idea— "the single best idea anyone has ever had," offered Daniel Dennett. Radiocarbon dating has revealed the antiquity of the earth and its fossil remains. Intermediate life forms have been discovered precisely where and when evolutionary theory has predicted. All life forms share a common language of life, which to the director of the Human Genome Project, Francis Collins, a self-described evangelical, is the exquisite "language of God." The DNA similarities across species extend even to nonfunctional "junk DNA" sequences that are shared by humans and mice. Moreover, the degree of DNA similarity among related species is, Collins notes, "exactly what Darwin's theory would predict." The "utterly compelling" evidence, he concludes, confirms that Darwin's idea is "unquestionably correct." Evolution was "God's elegant plan for creating humankind."

Collins' "theistic evolution" perspective has been shared by many kindred spirits throughout modern Christian history. In the biblical creation story, humankind is formed not out of nothing but from the earth itself—"the dust of the ground."

> Either half my colleagues are enormously stupid, or else the science of Darwinism is fully compatible with conventional religious beliefs—and equally compatible with atheism.
>
> —STEPHEN JAY GOULD, "IMPEACHING A SELF-APPOINTED JUDGE" (1992)

- In the fifth century, Saint Augustine ventured that "the universe was brought into being in a less than fully formed state but was gifted with the capacity to transform itself from unformed matter into a truly marvelous array of structures and life forms."

- A century ago, the conservative Protestant theologian Benjamin Warfield welcomed evolution as "a theory of the method of the divine providence."

- Theodosius Dobzhansky's famous quote, "Nothing in biology makes sense except in the light of evolution," came from a renowned biologist who was also a devout Eastern Orthodox Christian.

- Pope John Paul II in 1996 welcomed a science-religion dialogue, finding it noteworthy that evolutionary theory "has been progressively accepted by researchers, following a series of discoveries in various fields of knowledge."

- "Evolution describes the fundamental laws of nature according to which God chose to unfold life," offered Martin Nowak, the director of Harvard's Program for Evolutionary Dynamics in 2007.

- "The evidence for evolution can be fully compatible with religious faith," declared a 2008 National Academy of Sciences report, chaired by the evolutionary biologist and former Domincan priest Francisco Ayala. "Science and religion are different ways of understanding the world. Needlessly placing them in opposition reduces the potential of each to contribute to a better future."

"How nice," you say, "but these science-affirming people of faith are offset by the many scientifically illiterate Christians who think otherwise." Indeed, such folks are likely the majority of the 43 percent of Americans who in 2007 told Gallup that "God created human beings pretty much in their present form at one time within the last 10,000 years or so." A follow-up 2007 *Newsweek* survey reported this to be the belief of 73 percent of "evangelical Protestants" (though of only about 40 percent of Catholics and nonevangelical Protestants).

Some conservative Christians, few of whom are active scientific researchers, have offered "young earth creationist" and "intelligent design" alternatives. But they embarrass themselves and their faith, says fellow evangelical Francis Collins. Regarding the creationists, Collins notes that "all of the radioactive decay clocks, all the fossils, and all of the genome sequences" would have had to have been intentionally designed to mislead us into thinking the world was old when really it was created less than ten thousand years ago. How odd of God if he were to be the great deceiver, adds Collins (who has traveled Dawkins' theism-to-atheism journey in reverse). And how inconsistent with everything else the Bible indicates about God's love and logic.

Intelligent design theory grants the antiquity of the universe but contends that evolution cannot account for the complex human organism. Instead, it offers a God-of-the-gaps, an intelligent designer who intervened in the creation and tinkered with its inadequacies in order to generate life's complexity. But the assumed gaps that intelligent design seeks to fill are steadily being filled by scientific advances. For example, the oft-cited human eye, an engineering marvel, has its building blocks scattered around in other animals, enabling nature to select mutations that over time improve its design. As science progressively explains such complexities, it shrinks the gaps to which divine action can be attributed. Thus, notes Collins, intelligent design, like creationism, "is ironically on a path toward doing considerable damage to faith." (For more reflections on intelligent design, see the International Society for Science and Religion's 2008 statement in the Appendix.)

That is why many of us people of faith share your dismay over the seeming scientific illiteracy. Yet we also find in nature glimpses of transcendent genius. If you are open to being awestruck, lie back on a starry night and contemplate two weird and wonderful aspects of our scientific worldview.

One has been a great discovery that overturned the previous scientific understanding that the universe is without beginning and end, with energy preserved in a steady state. (If the universe has always existed then, as atheists supposed, it was not created. It just is.) We now know that the universe has been flying apart from a momentous beginning that, reversing the time arrow, cosmologists estimate must have happened nearly 14 billion years ago. Space, time, and the laws of nature were somehow born out of nothing.

To those familiar with the Hebrew Scriptures ("In the beginning, God created the heavens and the earth"), news of the Big Bang came as no surprise. As the astrophysicist Robert Jastrow wrote in *God and the Astronomers*, "Now we see how the astronomical evidence leads to a biblical view of the origin of the world. The details differ, but the essential elements and the astronomical and biblical accounts of Genesis are the same; the chain of events leading to man commenced suddenly and sharply at a definite moment in time, in a flash of light and energy." "The best data we have," added Arno Penzias, the Nobel laureate codiscoverer of the cosmic radiation that confirmed the Big Bang, "are exactly what I would have predicted, had I nothing to go on but the five Books of Moses, the Psalms, the Bible as a whole." Out of nothing, miracle of miracles, came something. The mysterious source of that grand event is what awestruck people call "God."

If that is not sufficiently weird and wonderful, contemplate the universe's staggering biofriendliness, its miraculous-seeming congeniality to intelligent life. In *Just Six Numbers*, Britain's Astronomer Royal, Sir Martin Rees, described six physical numbers that, if changed ever so slightly, would produce a universe inhospitable to life. If nature had provided a universe with the speed of light a teensy bit faster or slower, or had the carbon proton weighed infinitesimally more or less, you wouldn't be reading these words (which wouldn't exist to be read). In *Cosmic Jackpot: Why Our Universe Is Just Right for Life*, the cosmologist Paul Davies identifies many more physical constants, all of which, if there was to be a stable, biofriendly universe, needed to be precisely what they are. He notes that the chance likelihood of one "big fix," the value of "dark energy," "is like getting heads [in a coin toss] no fewer than *four hundred times in a row*. If the existence of life in the universe is . . . just a coincidence—then those are the odds against our being here. That level of flukiness seems too much to swallow."

In his poetic book *God's Universe*, the Harvard astronomer Owen Gingerich explains:

> I can recall vividly, from the time I was a young postdoc, the point when astronomers began to appreciate one of the most astonishing features of this cosmic event, the incredible balance between the outward energy of expansion and the gravitational forces trying to pull everything back together again. Because in the expansion itself any slight imbalance in either direction would be hugely magnified, the initial balance had to be accurate to about one part in 10^{59}—a ratio of 1 to 1-followed-by-fifty-nine-zeros, an unimaginably large number. Had the original energy of the Big Bang explosion been less, the universe would have fallen back in on itself long before there was time to build the elements required

not just get a diffret univer
- no univese
- no stds or peble!

for life and to produce from them intelligent,
sentient beings. Had the energy been greater,
it is quite likely that the density, and hence the
gravitational pull, of matter would have diminished
too swiftly for stars and galaxies to form. The balance
between the energy of expansion and the braking
power of gravitation had to be extraordinarily
exact—to such a degree that it seems as if the
universe must have been expressly designed for life.

So fine-tuned for life is our cosmos that it seems,
in the words of the physicist Freeman Dyson, "that
the universe in some sense must have known we were
coming."

So what shall we make of this? Were we just
extraordinarily, incomprehensibly lucky? The utter
improbability of our biofriendly universe makes that an
unsatisfying answer. One alternative to the religious idea
of a creative benevolent power is the conjecture that ours
is but one of an infinite number of spawned universes—
that rarest of universes that just happens to have all the
precise physical constants needed for biofriendliness.
But this "multiverse" conjecture of a meaningless,
accidental universe among zillions of wasted universes is
as much a statement of faith as the God hypothesis of a
meaningful, created universe (not to mention a seeming
violation of Occam's razor, the principle that we should

A FRIENDLY LETTER TO SKEPTICS AND ATHEISTS

prefer the simplest of competing explanations). And it leaves unanswered the ultimate question: Why is there something rather than nothing?

The possibility that the universe was intentionally created, adds Gingerich, suggests a final cause that transcends scientific explanation. Gingerich, who believes that a superintelligent Creator exists beyond and within the cosmos, also

> Science reveals just what a marvel the universe is . . . a coherent, rational, elegant, and harmonious expression of a deep and purposeful meaning.
>
> —PAUL DAVIES, "GLIMPSING THE MIND OF GOD" (2006)

believes that science offers explanations of how things work, though not necessarily why they work. Science suggests the physics. Genesis suggests the metaphysics.

Big Ideas and Biblical Wisdom

From what we have just seen, many scientists comfortably reconcile their theism with their cosmology or evolutionary biology. But what about my neck of the scientific woods, psychology?

In any academic field, the results of thousands of studies, the conclusions of hundreds of investigators, and the insights of dozens of theorists can often be boiled down to a few overriding ideas. Biology offers us principles such as natural selection and adaptation. Sociology builds on concepts such as social structure, cultural relativity, and social organization. Music exploits our ideas of rhythm, melody, and harmony.

My specialty—social psychology—is the same. I see four really big ideas about human nature that are rooted in science *and* are congenial with Judeo-Christian understandings. In each instance, science does not discount religious wisdom—it affirms it. And each is a two-sided truth. As Blaise Pascal reminded us three hundred years ago, no single truth is ever sufficient, because the world is not simple. Any truth separated from its complementary truth is a half-truth.

1. *Our cognitive capacities are awesome. But to err is human.* How "noble in reason!" and "infinite in faculties!" rhapsodized Shakespeare's Hamlet about the human intellect. In some ways, indeed, *our cognitive capacities are awesome.* The three pounds of tissue in our skulls contain circuitry more complex than all the phone networks on the planet, enabling us to process information automatically, to soak up the more than sixty thousand words in our vocabulary, to remember vast quantities of information, and to make snap intuitive judgments.

Jewish and Christian theologians have long agreed that we *are* awesome. We are *made in the divine image* and given stewardship of the earth and its creatures. We are the summit of the Creator's work, God's own children.

Yet our *explanations and social judgments are vulnerable to error,* insist social psychologists. When observing others, we are sometimes too prone to let our preconceptions bias our responses. We "see" illusory relationships and causes. We treat people in ways that trigger them to fulfill our expectations. We are swayed more by vivid anecdotes than by statistical reality. We attribute others' behavior to their dispositions (as when presuming that someone who acts strangely must be strange). Failing to recognize such errors in our thinking, we are prone to overconfident judgments.

Such conclusions have a familiar ring to theologians, who have reminded us that *we are finite creatures* of the One who declares "I am God, and there is none like me" and that "as the heavens are higher than the earth, so are my ways higher than your ways and my thoughts higher than your thoughts." Thus we must be skeptical of those who claim for themselves godlike powers of omniscience (reading others' minds, foretelling the future), omnipresence (viewing happenings in remote locations), and omnipotence (creating or altering physical reality with mental power). We should be wary even of those who idolize their religion, presuming their doctrinal fine points to be absolute truth. "If we have understood, then what we have understood is not God," cautioned Augustine. Always, we see reality through a dim mirror. Religion that forgets this is, indeed, religion that is vulnerable to becoming delusional and dangerous.

2. *Self-serving pride is powerful and perilous. Yet self-acceptance pays dividends.* Even when we think we're being completely truthful with and about ourselves, we usually aren't. Heeding the ancient admonition to "know thyself," we analyze our behavior, but not impartially. Our tendency to fool ourselves appears in our differing explanations for our successes and failures, for our good

deeds and bad. On any socially desirable dimension, we commonly exhibit a "self-serving bias." We view ourselves as relatively superior—as more ethical, more socially skilled, and more tolerant than our average peer. (More than 90 percent of drivers judge themselves as "better than average.") Moreover, we justify our past behaviors. We have an inflated confidence in the accuracy of our beliefs. We misremember our own past in self-enhancing ways. And we overestimate how virtuously we would behave in difficult or challenging situations that draw less than virtuous behavior out of most people.

The social psychological conclusion that we experience life through a self-centered filter echoes a very old religious idea: *self-righteous pride is the fundamental sin*, the original sin, the deadliest of the seven deadly sins. Thus the psalmist could declare that "no one can see his own errors" and the Pharisee could sanctimoniously thank God "that I am not like other men" (and you and I can thank God that we are not like the Pharisee). Pride goes before a fall. It corrodes our relations with one another, as in conflicts between marriage partners, between management and labor, between nations or tribes at war. Each side views its motives alone as pure, its actions beyond reproach. Alas, so does its antagonist.

Yet self-affirmation pays dividends. It helps maintain our confidence and minimize our depression. To doubt our efficacy and to blame ourselves solely for our mistakes is a recipe for failure, loneliness, or depression. People made to feel secure and valued exhibit less prejudice and contempt for others.

Again, there is a religious parallel. To sense divine grace—the Christian parallel to psychology's "unconditional positive regard"—is to be liberated from both self-protective pride and self-condemnation. To feel profoundly affirmed, just as I am, lessens my need to define my self-worth in terms of achievements, prestige, or material and physical well-being. It's rather like insecure Pinocchio saying to his maker Geppetto, "Papa, I am not sure who I am. But if I'm all right with you, then I guess I'm all right with me."

3. *Attitudes and beliefs influence behavior. And attitudes and beliefs follow behavior.* Studies during the 1960s shocked social psychologists with revelations that our attitudes sometimes lie dormant, overwhelmed by other influences. But follow-up research was reassuring. *Our attitudes influence our behavior*—when they are relevant and brought to mind. Thus our political attitudes influence how we vote. Our smoking attitudes influence our susceptibility to peer pressures to smoke. Change the way people think, and whether we call such persuasion "education" or "propaganda," the impact may be considerable.

If social psychology has taught us anything, it is that the reverse is also true: we are as likely to *act* ourselves into a way of thinking as to think ourselves into action. We are as likely to believe in what we have stood up for as to stand up for what we believe. Especially when we feel responsible for how we have acted, our behaviors influence our attitudes. This self-persuasion enables all sorts of people—political campaigners, lovers, even terrorists—to believe more strongly in that for which they have testified or suffered. Attitudes follow behavior.

The realization of the intimate, reciprocal relationship between inner attitude and outer behavior parallels the Jewish-Christian idea that inner faith and outer action feed one another. Thus faith is a source of action. Elijah is overwhelmed by the Holy as he huddles in a cave. Paul is transformed on the Damascus Road. Ezekiel, Isaiah, and Jeremiah undergo an inner transformation. In each case, a new spiritual consciousness produces a new pattern of behavior.

But faith is also a consequence of action. Throughout the Old and New Testaments, faith is seen as nurtured by obedient action. The Old Testament Hebrew word for know is usually a verb, something one does. To know love, one must not only know about love but also act lovingly. Philosophers and theologians note how faith grows as people act on whatever faith they have. In the Jewish tradition, rabbis were taught to tell their people that the act of praying would help grow their belief. "The proof of Christianity really consists in 'following,'" declared the Christian philosopher Søren Kierkegaard. C. S. Lewis concurred: "Believe in God and you will have to face hours when it

> Follow the way by which [the committed] began; by acting as if they believed, taking the holy water, having masses said, etc. Even this will naturally make you believe. . . .
>
> —BLAISE PASCAL, *PENSÉES* (1669)

seems *obvious* that this material world is the only reality; disbelieve in Him and you must face hours when this material world seems to shout at you that it is not all. No conviction, religious or irreligious, will, of itself, end once and for all [these doubts] in the soul. Only the practice of Faith resulting in the habit of Faith will gradually do that."

4. *We are the creatures—and the creators—of our social worlds.* My final two-sided truth is that people interact with their situations. We see this, first, in the evidence that social influences powerfully affect our behavior. As vividly shown in studies of conformity, role playing, persuasion, and group influence, *we are the creatures of our social worlds.*

The most dramatic findings come from experiments that put well-intentioned people in morally challenging situations to see whether good or evil prevailed. To a dismaying extent, evil pressures overwhelm good intentions, inducing people to conform to falsehoods or capitulate to cruelty (as they did with the abuses at Iraq's Abu Ghraib prison, for example). Faced with an intimidating situation, nice people often don't behave so nicely. Depending on the social context, most of us are capable of acting kindly or brutally, independently or submissively, wisely or foolishly. In one irony-laden experiment, most Princeton Seminary students en route to recording an extemporaneous talk on the Good Samaritan parable failed to stop and aid a slumped, groaning person—*if* they had been pressed to hurry. External social forces powerfully shape our social behavior.

The social psychological concept of powers greater than the individual parallels the religious idea of *transcendent good and evil powers*, with evil symbolized in the creation story as a seductive serpent. Evil involves not only individual rotten apples here and there. It also is a product of "principalities and powers"—corrosive forces—that can ruin a whole barrel of apples.

Although powerful situations may override people's individual dispositions, social psychologists do not view humans as passive tumbleweeds, blown this way and that by the social winds. Facing the same situation, different people may react differently, depending on their personality and culture. When some feel coerced by blatant pressure, they will sometimes react in ways that restore their sense of freedom. In a numerical minority, they will sometimes oppose and sway the majority. When they believe in themselves and their own agency, they sometimes work wonders. In study after study, those who feel in control of their lives (as assessed on a measure of "internal locus of control") achieve more in school, act more independently, enjoy better health, more effectively delay gratification, and feel less depressed than their peers who feel that their lives are externally controlled. Measures that increase control—allowing prisoners to move chairs and to control room lights and TV, having workers participate in decision making, offering nursing home patients choices about their environment—noticeably improve health and morale. (No wonder I love my TiVo.) Moreover, in everyday life, we often choose our situations—our college environments, our jobs, our locales. And our social expectations are sometimes self-fulfilling, as when we expect someone to be warm or hostile and, sure enough, they become so. In such ways, we are the creators of our social worlds.

To most religious traditions, that rings true. We are morally responsible—accountable for how we use whatever freedom we have. What we decide matters. The stream of causation from past to future runs through our choices.

Faced with these four pairs of complementary ideas, framed either psychologically or theologically, we are like someone stranded in a deep well with two rope ends dangling within reach. If we grab either one alone, we sink deeper into the well. Only when we grasp both ropes can we climb out, because at the top, beyond where we can see, they come together around a pulley. Grabbing only the rope of rationality or irrationality, of humility or self-esteem, of attitudes first or behavior first, of personal or situational causation, plunges us to the bottom of the well. So we grab both ropes, perhaps without fully understanding how they come together. In doing so, we may be comforted that in both science and religion, accepting complementary principles is sometimes more honest than an oversimplified theory that ignores half the evidence. For the scissors of truth, we need both blades.

Secularism and Civility

Even granting a certain congeniality between some big ideas in psychological science and biblical religion, you might ask, "If you think faith is good for us, then imagine this: you are about to be uprooted and dropped into a new place. You are hoping it will be a safe, civil, humane, harmonious, healthy country or state, a place where people flourish. Given a choice between a random secular or religious place, which would most likely fulfill your hopes?"

Is the Family Research Council right to promote "the Judeo-Christian worldview as the basis for a just, free and stable society"? Was Dostoyevsky right to suppose that "if God does not exist, then everything is permissible"? Does predominantly Christian America reflect John Winthrop's (and Ronald Reagan's) vision of "a shining city on a hill"? Reject God and suffer the ills, say the faith-heads. Crime, poverty, divorce, and rampant disease will be the natural result.

If that is true, then highly religious nations—and highly religious American states—should be notably stable, peaceful, healthy, and flourishing. But it just isn't so. Indeed, the most challenging evidence I have encountered in preparing this book is the hard reality that the countries with the highest life expectancy, literacy, income, gender equality, and education and the lowest infant morality, homicide, AIDS, and teen pregnancy rates are relatively secular. If you want your new location to be a civil, safe, healthy place, you might hope to be plopped into relatively irreligious Norway, Sweden, Australia, Canada, or the Netherlands.

Analysts of secularity and civility have been faulted for cherry-picking both their social health measures (for example, excluding burglary rates) and their countries. The analyses conveniently omit antireligious North Korea, China, Vietnam, and the former Soviet states. Instead, they focus on secular countries whose values were fed by a Christian heritage and the Protestant ethic.

Still, one can find correlates of religiosity and social pathology across the United States as well. To document the skeptics' point, I obtained state-by-state "religious adherence rates" (which I take to be a rough proxy for what is seemingly unavailable: state-by-state religious engagement assessed as worship attendance rates). For example, is what you may have heard true—that as the Barna Research Group claimed in 1999, religious people have a *higher* divorce rate? As a simple first look, I compared two cultures within the United States: the relatively religious southern states and the more irreligious West Coast states. As Figure 1 shows, the southern states have a strikingly higher rate of religious adherence and a slightly higher divorce rate.

FIGURE 1. Religious Adherents and Divorce Rates, Selected States. Source: Association of Religious Data Archives.

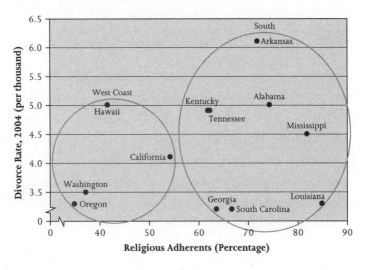

Of course, state-by-state and country-by-country analyses compare more than religiosity. Such places also differ in education, income, and age of marriage—all of which are major predictors of long-term marital success. In comparing Swedes and Americans, or those in southern and West Coast states, we compare groups with differing histories, racial makeup, schooling, and lots more, including religiousness.

So let's ask whether religiously active individuals divorce more often. The rubber meets the road in the form of personal religious beliefs, values, and social behavior. To compare individuals, I accessed the University of Chicago's National Opinion Research Center data archives. The center's periodic General Social Survey is the most comprehensive national sampling of representative Americans, with some forty-six thousand randomly sampled people responding to their many questions since 1972. So are the most religiously active people the most likely to divorce?

As you can see in Figure 2, compared to people who never attend religious services, weekly religious attenders are markedly more likely to be married and *half as likely* to be divorced. So much for the idea of divorce-prone faith-heads.

FIGURE 2. Religious Attendance and Marital Status, 1972–2004.
Source: National Opinion Research Center.

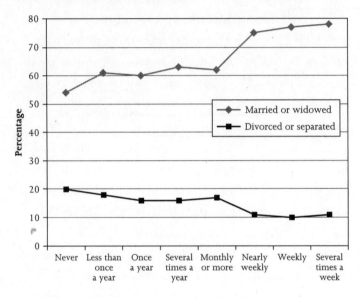

Let's test the secularism hypothesis again, with a health-related factor. Are people in the more religious South more likely than West Coasters to practice slow-motion suicide by smoking? As Figure 3 shows, the comparison of the two regions is striking. The lowest smoking rate among these religious southern states exceeds the highest smoking rate among the more irreligious West Coast states. By this measure, secular states are healthy states.

FIGURE 3. Smoking Rate and Religious Adherence, Selected States.
Sources: Centers for Disease Control and Prevention; Association of Religious
Data Archives.

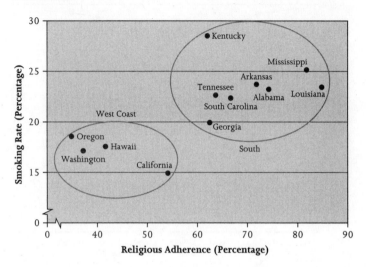

But again, we're not only comparing more versus less religious places but also regions with differing education, races, income levels, and so forth. Education, for example, is a huge predictor of nonsmoking. (Among Americans in their early twenties, more than half of high school dropouts smoke, as do barely one in ten college grads.) So I visited the General Social Survey archives again to see the correlation of religiosity with smoking across individuals; the results are presented in Figure 4.

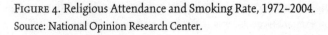

FIGURE 4. Religious Attendance and Smoking Rate, 1972–2004.
Source: National Opinion Research Center.

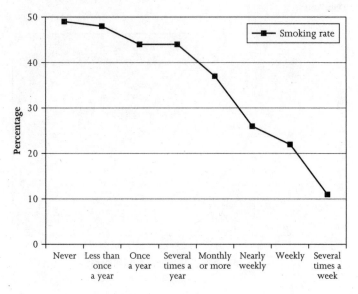

Like education, religious engagement is a visibly huge predictor of *not* smoking. And though I have no data to verify it, I would wager the value of my house that Judeo-Christian religious engagement is also a predictor of nonsmoking in any state or local context.

Let's give the secularity-civility correlation one more test by examining whether religious or secular places have higher crime rates. As Figure 5 shows, once again, the comparison of southern and West Coast cultures confirms the skeptics' observation that secular places are civil places. But once again, the regions differ

FIGURE 5. Crime Rate and Religious Attendance, Selected States. Sources: Federal Bureau of Investigation; Association of Religious Data Archives.

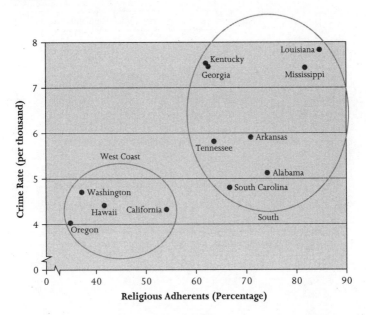

in education, income, race, social history, and so forth. And what we'd really like to know is whether highly religious *individuals* are more or less likely to have been arrested. Thanks to the data archive, we do know; the results are presented in Figure 6.

So there is pretty strong evidence to support the argument that secular places (at least in Christian-heritage democratic societies) tend to be civil places, thanks partly to their educated, higher-income populations. Nevertheless, in the cultural contexts

FIGURE 6. Religious Attendance and Arrest Rate, 1972–2004.
Source: National Opinion Research Center.

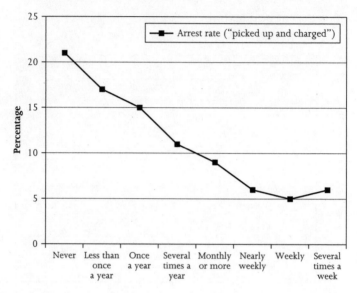

sampled, faith-active individuals are *less* likely to divorce, smoke, and be arrested.

The religiosity-civility correlation does not prove that religious engagement is the positive causal factor. (Maybe religion rides along with some other causal factor, or maybe nonsmoking, law-abiding, married people seek out faith communities.) But the correlation does appear in specific subgroups, as, for example, in the arrest rates of individuals with lots of education and those with little, of black folks and of white folks, of men and of women. Ditto for the correlation between religious engagement and marriage, which also exists in different population groups. This much, then, can be said: these correlations are comfortably consistent with the idea that faith fosters fidelity.

We've only scratched the surface (with lots more evidence to come). But let me offer a thought in the spirit of your question. If you think faith is bad for us, then imagine this: late on a Friday night, you are walking alone down a deserted city street. Several older teen males emerge from a building you have just passed and start walking behind you. Based on these data and on what your gut tells you, would you feel more or less threatened if you knew that they were leaving a Bible study class?

God and Gays

Even if I were to persuade you of a deep congeniality
between scientific and Christian understandings of
the cosmos and of human nature, and even if I were
to convince you that an active faith restrains divorce,
smoking, crime, and other antisocial behaviors, you
would likely still recoil when encountering religion-
justified homophobia and racial and gender prejudice.
Be assured, many of us faith-heads also recoil. Here, as
with understandings of evolution, there is a huge gulf
between the assumptions and attitudes of scientists
(including academic psychologists who are people of
faith) and those of many Christians. And here again, that
wisdom of Proverbs (19:2) applies: "It is not good to
have zeal without knowledge."

Recognizing that the church is ground zero for
the gay marriage debate, and hoping to contribute
information to that conversation, Letha Dawson Scanzoni
and I recently wrote a short book, *What God Has Joined
Together: The Christian Case for Gay Marriage*. Understanding

why Elton John might think that religion promotes spite toward gays and "turns people into hateful lemmings," we wanted to reassure you, our secular friends, that Christianity is not intrinsically antagonistic to gays and lesbians. But our main goal was to help bridge the divide between marriage-supporting and gay-supporting people of faith by documenting the following assertions:

• *All humans have a deep "need to belong,"* to connect with others in close, intimate, enduring relationships. We are, as Aristotle recognized long ago, "the social animal." Solitary confinement, ostracism, and banishment from close relationships lead to genuine pain. Show social scientists a community where marriages are plentiful, and they will show you a community with mostly healthy and happy people, thriving kids, and low crime rates. Celebrities who really care about children (Angelina Jolie and Brad Pitt come to mind) could exemplify the social ecology that best nurtures youth: by marrying their partners. They could model the message that *marriage matters.*

• *Radical individualism and the media modeling of impulsive sexuality are corroding marriage and the health of communities.* There is ample evidence to support these contentions. As I documented in an earlier book, *The American Paradox: Spiritual Hunger in an Age of Plenty,* there is a social cost to focusing on "me" to the exclusion of "we" and to modeling sexuality and its consequences as mere recreation rather than as a life-uniting, love-renewing force.

• *Sexual orientation is not a personal choice,* but rather a natural (largely biologically influenced) disposition, most clearly so for men. A host of recent neuroscience studies offer a dozen you-never-would-have-guessed discoveries of gay-straight differences in traits ranging from fingerprint patterns to hair whorl direction to skill at mentally rotating geometric figures.

• *Sexual orientation is an enduring disposition* that is seldom reversed by willpower, reparative therapy, or ex-gay ministry. "Can therapy change sexual orientation?" asks an American Psychological Association statement. "No. [It] is not changeable." There are anecdotes of ex-gays, but these are offset by anecdotes of ex-ex-gays—often the same people a few years later. And claims of "healing" are becoming fewer and more modest.

• *The Bible has nothing to say about an enduring sexual orientation* (a modern concept) or about loving, long-term same-sex partnerships. Out of 31,103 Bible verses, only seven frequently quoted verses (none the words of Jesus) speak directly of same-sex behavior—and mostly in the context of idolatry, temple prostitution, adultery, child exploitation, or violence. By contrast, noted the Christian humanitarian rocker Bono in his 2006 National Prayer Breakfast talk, "poverty is mentioned more than 2,100 times. . . . That's a lot of air time." Be assured, my skeptical friends, the church's distraction over a very few debatable verses—mere needles in the haystack of biblical teachings—does not represent the priorities of Jesus.

• *There is a Christian case for gay marriage*, which arises from the human need to belong, from the biblical mandate for justice, from the benefits of a culturewide norm of monogamy, and from a refutation of popular arguments against gay marriage.

"Whoa!" say critics on the religious right. "By encouraging 'open and affirming' attitudes, you are aiding the spread of homosexuality!" To check this presumption—that social attitudes influence sexual orientation—I retrieved National Opinion Research Center data from 1988 and then from 2004 (after sixteen years of visibly increased acceptance of gays and lesbians in the media and in various vocations). In 1988, when the question was first asked with procedures that assured anonymity, 97 percent of sexually active males reported having exclusively female partners during the previous year. In 2004, the most recent year for which data are available, the result was still 97 percent. (Among sexually active females, 99 percent in 2004 reported

having exclusively male partners during the previous
year.) Today's more open and affirming attitudes seem
not to be influencing the population's sexual orientation.

So we say to our fellow people of faith: should we
not put on our social radar screens the concerns that
Jesus had on his? What *would* Jesus do? Rather than tie
"onto people's backs loads that are heavy and hard to
carry," as Jesus said of the Pharisees, why not offer a
positive affirmation of monogamy? Why not stand up
for healthy relationships that satisfy the human need
to belong within covenant partnerships? Rather than
advocating a sexual double standard for straight people
(marry or be celibate) and gay people (sorry, you must
be celibate), why not proclaim a single Christian sexual
ethic? Why not yoke sex with faithfulness? Why not seal
love with commitment? Why not foster a conservative,
marriage-supporting positive argument: that the world
would be a happier and healthier place if, *for all people,*
sex, love, and marriage routinely went together?

Genuine biblical priorities may be something other
than what we Christians sometimes propound. The Bible
is like the U.S. Constitution: it says many things clearly,
and these form the agreed foundation of our communal
life while leaving us to argue its implications for many
other issues. For the Bible's minor topics (those with but
a few debated verses set in a particular cultural context),
it is tempting to project one's ideas into God's mouth,

thus making the Bible say what we believe. When you catch us doing this, call us on it.

The influence of one's preconceptions on biblical interpretation is no surprise to anyone familiar with psychological research. Our expectations and "mental sets" can powerfully predispose what we perceive and how we interpret the world around us. To believe is to see. For example,

> We hear and apprehend only what we already half know.
>
> —HENRY DAVID THOREAU, JOURNAL ENTRY, JAN. 5, 1860

after presidential debates, partisans overwhelmingly perceive their candidate as having won. A 1995 Gallup Poll found that after hearing much the same evidence, 78 percent of blacks but only 42 percent of whites approved O. J. Simpson's "not guilty" verdict. We view reality through the spectacles of our beliefs, attitudes, and values. This is one reason why our beliefs are important: they shape our interpretation of everything else.

If the Bible actually has little, if anything, directly to say about sexual orientation and loving, committed, same-sex partnerships, and if faithful Christians disagree about the few pertinent biblical texts, then, you may wonder, why is the church so preoccupied with this issue (as opposed, say, to concern for justice, the poor, and our stewardship of the creation, about which the Bible has so much to say)?

The University of Virginia social psychologist Jonathan Haidt suggests an explanation for the church's current preoccupation. Often, his research shows, the rationalist idea that we reason our way to moral judgments has it backward. Instead, we make instant gut-level moral judgments and then seek rationalizations for our feelings (another example of emotions feeding thinking). Many people, he finds, will feel instant disgust over an objectively harmless but degrading behavior, such as scrubbing a toilet with the flag, and will then mentally scramble to construct moral reasons that support their moral intuition. First come the feelings, then the rationalization.

Recent studies have similarly found that prejudice arises less from cerebral justifications than from automatic, gut-level reactions that seek justification. Reason is often the slave of passion. Moral reasoning therefore aims to convince others of what we intuitively feel, which in times past has led people to find in the Bible ample support for the subordination of African Americans and women. Haidt's research also helps us understand why surveys find that people with gay friends come to have more accepting attitudes and also to have more supportive opinions about gay rights and gay marriage. (As empathy replaces disgust, one's rationalizations change.) And no wonder men—who, more than women, feel disgust over same-sex relationships—write most of the antigay tracts.

Those of us who support an inclusive pro-monogamy norm can take heart that more and more people see the welcoming of gay people into monogamy—into marriage—as a positive trend while also seeing declines in teen pregnancy and increases in teen abstinence as positive trends. Marriage nevertheless is in trouble. With the marriage rate having declined, with most first marriages preceded by cohabitation, with 39 percent of American children in 2006 born outside of marriage, and with pornography a bigger business than professional football, there is surely a need to refocus on the family. Alas, rather than focus on getting and keeping people married, the church is diverting its energy into keeping gay people unmarried. One is reminded of senior devil Screwtape's advice (in C. S. Lewis' *Screwtape Letters*) on how to corrupt: "The game is to have them all running about with fire extinguishers whenever there is a flood."

✳ MARRIAGE.

(Nominal) Religion Feeds Prejudice

Hostility towards gays is hardly the only way Christians have failed to follow Jesus' great commandment to "love your neighbor as yourself." Indeed, every ideology is plagued by those whose behavior defames it. Thus every religious skeptic, and also every believer, can point to those who profess love and practice hate.

 It won't surprise religious skeptics to learn that in twentieth-century surveys, American church members, on average, expressed more racial prejudice than nonmembers. Moreover, those professing traditional Christian beliefs have expressed more racial prejudice than those with less traditional beliefs. In *The End of Faith*, Sam Harris surmises that such intolerance extends to people with different beliefs: "Certainty about the next life is simply incompatible with tolerance in this one."

We faith-heads also must acknowledge that throughout history, religion has provided convenient excuses—indeed, powerful justifications—for all sorts of cruelty: the horrors of military crusades, the dehumanization of slavery and apartheid, the subordination of women, to name just three. The beautiful

> *Men never do evil so completely and cheerfully as when they do it from religious conviction.*
>
> —BLAISE PASCAL, PENSÉES (1669)

medieval town of Saint Andrews, where I have spent many months, was Scotland's ecclesiastical center before the Protestant Reformation. In the year 1643 alone, forty terrified women were judged by church elders to be witches and consigned to torture and death. These and other religious martyrs remind us that behind religious fanaticism, evil often lurks. Jesus reserved some of his strongest condemnation for the self-righteous religious folk of his day. From his time to ours, "not everyone who says . . . 'Lord, Lord'" speaks for God.   — nt 6

Nevertheless, religion's links with prejudice seem paradoxical. As the psychologist Gordon Allport noted more than half a century ago, "It makes prejudice and it unmakes prejudice." The unmaking of prejudice is suggested first by studies that compared strongly engaged with less engaged church members. In nearly every one of more than two dozen studies, faithful church attenders exhibited less prejudice than irregular attenders. This even appears true in that oft-used example of religious toxicity, Northern Ireland, where "Protestant" and "Catholic" function as ethnic markers. When I asked Ed Cairns, a distinguished social psychologist who leads the University of Ulster's Peace and Conflict Research Group, about whether survey data indicated that religious devoutness or frequent church attendance predicted more hostile attitudes, he told me, "If anything, the more people believed or went to church, the less prejudice they showed."

Second, those for whom religion is an end in itself (the "intrinsically religious" who agree, for example, with the statement "My religious beliefs are what really lie behind my whole approach of life") typically express less racial prejudice than the "extrinsically religious"— those for whom religion is more a means to other ends (for example, who agree with the statement "A primary reason for my interest in religion is that my church is a congenial social activity").

Third, ministers and priests (who presumably are more religiously committed and motivated than most people) have also generally been more supportive of civil rights efforts than their own laypeople have. So it seems that among the churched, the devout exhibit less prejudice and deeper feelings of human kinship than the nominally religious, who are somewhat more likely to rationalize prejudice with the aid of religion. Prejudice arises less from too much religious devotion than from too much mindless, nominal religion.

Here, then, one finds support for the contention that religion is dangerous: *A little religion is indeed sometimes a*

> We have just enough religion to make us hate, but not enough to make us love one another.
>
> —JONATHAN SWIFT, *THOUGHTS OF VARIOUS SUBJECTS* (1711)

dangerous thing. Moreover, fundamentalism can feed on faith. What better way to justify one's own antagonism than to fashion "God" in our ideological image? Tribalism plus theism equals arrogance. Multiplied times two, it often equals violent conflict between two groups who each think God is with them. Yet the mark of authentic religion, certainly for followers of Jesus,   — James
is not dogmatism and hostility but humility and charity, as dramatically evident in the forgiveness and grace the Amish community displayed after the 2006 massacre of five girls at a one-room Pennsylvania Amish school.

What, then, might be the Christian response to bigots and their bigotry? First, reject the sin and love the sinner. Hate the bigotry and love the bigot. Be intolerant of intolerance, despise lovelessness, detest injustice, and remember, "The fruit of the spirit is love, joy, peace,   Gal 5:22
patience, kindness, goodness, faithfulness, gentleness, and self-control."

Second, take heart from those heroes of the faith who exemplify such fruit. If we are most troubled by the small-mindedness of those whose lives seem to deny the good news message of love, peace, and reconciliation, we are also most encouraged by those whose lives witness to the power of deep faith. It was Quakers and evangelicals such as Thomas Clarkson and William Wilberforce whose faith-inspired values motivated their following Jesus' second commandment ("love your neighbor as yourself") with a successful campaign to end slavery and the slave trade in the British Empire. It was ministers who provided much of the leadership for the later American abolitionist and South African antiapartheid movements. It was a young Martin Luther King Jr. who sermonized in Montgomery, Alabama, that "standing up for the truth of God is the greatest thing in the world. . . . The end of life is to do the will of God, come what may." Only through spiritual transformation, he said, "do we gain the strength to fight vigorously the evils of the world in a humble and loving spirit."

CIVIL
RIGHTS
LEADER

Godliness and Goodliness

Granted, you say, Christianity can point to those who
exemplify its aspirations—to its Martin Luther Kings and
William Wilberforces, its Mother Teresas and Desmond
Tutus, its Miltons and
Michelangelos. You
may acknowledge
or even admire
the countless

> Christians have given Christianity a
> bad name.
>
> —MADELINE L'ENGLE, *WALKING ON
> WATER* (1980)

hospitals, orphanages, hospices, and universities that
religious groups have established. But if we're going
to credit Christianity for its heroes, you say, should
we not also blame it for its horrors? For its Bible-
quoting KKKers and gay bashers? Its Crusades and
Inquisitions? Its genocide of Kosovo Muslims? It's
no stretch to understand why Christopher Hitchens
would give his book *God Is Not Great* the subtitle *How
Religion Poisons Everything*. Or why the cosmologist Steven
Weinberg would say that "anything that we scientists
can do to weaken the hold of religion should be done

and may in the end be our greatest contribution to civilization."

It all got even worse on September 11, 2001. The "insane courage" that enabled this horror "came from religion," noted Richard Dawkins in the *Manchester Guardian*. If "a martyr's death is equivalent to pressing the hyperspace button and zooming through a wormhole to another universe, it can make the world a very dangerous place. . . . To fill a world with religion, or religions of the Abrahamic kind, is like littering the streets with loaded guns."

Dawkins may be right that a warped religious idea of martyrdom and the afterlife was at work on those ill-fated flights. And he's surely right that religion at its worst can be toxic and superstitious—which is something healthy religion must be ever vigilant about (much as science is vigilant about pseudoscience). The vivid examples—the worst and the best—capture our attention but do not decide the issue. Those judgments find support in the Bible itself, where much of the Old and New Testaments are devoted to exploring and exposing how religion

> Organized religion has fostered, throughout Western history, both the most unspeakable horrors and the most heartrending example of human goodness.
>
> —STEPHEN JAY GOULD,
> "NONOVERLAPPING MAGISTERIA" (1997)

[handwritten margin note: EVIL DONE IN NAME OF SCIENCE | -EUGENICS -(NAZI)]

becomes toxic. Jesus' expressed contempt for the legalism of the Pharisees or the activities of the money-changers has perhaps put a nodding smile on the face of Richard Dawkins or Christopher Hitchens.

But on balance, is religion humane or heartless? Is Christianity, for example, a source more of compassion or is it, as Dawkins' British Channel 4 series proclaimed, "The root of all evil"? The extremes—the churchgoing civil rights activists and the churchgoing Ku Klux Klansmen—rhetorically cancel each other out. It remains for dispassionate research with ordinary people to help us decide the issue.

The evidence, I will suggest to you, my skeptic friends, is that Christianity has, on balance, proved more benevolent than malevolent. For serious followers of Jesus, the mandate is clear. Love God and neighbor. Like the Good Samaritan, give of yourself to strangers. Do good even to those who persecute you. And embody the unconventional values that Jesus taught at the beginning of his most famous sermon:

> Blessed are the poor in spirit, for theirs is the kingdom of heaven.
> Blessed are those who mourn, for they will be comforted.
> Blessed are the meek, for they will inherit the earth.

Blessed are those who hunger and thirst for
righteousness, for they will be filled.
Blessed are the merciful, for they will receive mercy.
Blessed are the pure in heart, for they will see God.
Blessed are the peacemakers, for they will be called
children of God.
Blessed are those who are persecuted for righteousness'
sake, for theirs is the kingdom of heaven.

Jesus' teaching finds a modern expression in
the 1986 Belhar Confession of the Uniting Reformed
Church in Southern Africa, which is en route to
being embraced by sister denominations, including
my own:

We believe
- that God has revealed himself as the One who
  wishes to bring about justice and true peace among
  people
- that God, in a world full of injustice and enmity, is in
  a special way the God of the destitute, the poor and
  the wronged
- that God calls the church to follow him in this, for
  God brings justice to the oppressed and gives bread
  to the hungry . . .
- that the church as the possession of God must stand
  where the Lord stands, namely, against injustice and
  with the wronged

- that in following Christ the church must witness against all the powerful and privileged who selfishly seek their own interests and thus control and harm others

Nice teachings, great values, you might say. But do they move people to walk the talk? Although the evidence I'm about to present doesn't verify religion's truth claims, it does challenge the presumption that the world would be a better place without religion.

A utopian vision. If human life and identity are believed to have value that make them worth preserving, and if one foresees a utopian afterlife marked by peace, justice, and love, then one may have a back-to-the-present vision

> Hope is hearing the melody of the future. Faith is to dance to it.
>
> —RUBEM ALVES, *TOMORROW'S CHILD* (1972)

for life on earth. Thus Martin Luther King Jr. could talk about his dream of a future reality without oppression and suffering. With a dream worth dying for and a hope that even death could not kill, he declared, "If physical death is the price I must pay to free my white brothers and sisters from a permanent death of the spirit, then nothing can be more redemptive."

Promoting positive virtues. Fundamentalist forms of religion often feed favoritism to in-groups and hostility toward out groups; the circle that defines "us" also defines "them." Yet most religions also advocate many of the human virtues championed by the burgeoning positive psychology movement, as in Christopher Peterson and Martin Seligman's *Character Strengths and Virtues* handbook and in C. R. Snyder and Shane Lopez's *Handbook of Positive Psychology*. (Positive psychologists study positive emotions and human strengths.) Moreover, note Peterson and Seligman, "religiousness, broadly speaking, also has been empirically linked to a range of human virtues, including forgiveness, kindness, and compassion."

Forgiveness. Forgiveness, or something close to it, is a shared feature of Judaism, Christianity, Islam, Buddhism, and Hinduism. Psychological researchers engaged in a recent wave of forgiveness studies agree that forgiveness does not deny, excuse, or forget wrongs. But it may cut short a cycle of violence by cultivating positive responses such as compassion that supplant hurtful and bitter thoughts and emotions. Forgiveness fosters reconciliation. And in both laboratory and clinical intervention studies, forgiveness predicts improved emotional and physical well-being.

Gratitude. Gratitude "is a felt sense of wonder, thankfulness, and appreciation for life," say Robert Emmons and Charles Shelton. Much as rumination prolongs and intensifies depression, so counting one's blessings enhances well-being. Students asked to keep a weekly log of things for which they are grateful come to "feel better about their lives as a whole," report Emmons and Shelton. Ditto for those who kept daily gratitude logs. Emmons and Shelton note that gratitude is highly valued in Jewish, Christian, Muslim, Buddhist, and Hindu thought and is found in texts, prayers, and teachings of all those religions. "Those who regularly attend religious services and engage in religious activities such as prayer or reading religious material are more likely to be grateful," add Peterson and Seligman.

Compassion. Compassion and its associated "kindness, generosity, nurturance, care, . . . and altruistic love" are positive character traits that orient "the self toward the other," report Peterson and Seligman. Shalom Schwartz and Sipke Huismans explored such norms among Jews in Israel, Catholics in Spain, Calvinists in the Netherlands, the Orthodox in Greece, and Lutherans and Catholics in western Germany. In each place, they found highly religious people to be less hedonistic and self-oriented. Faith-rooted values give many people a reason to behave morally when no one is looking. "Religions encourage people to seek meaning beyond everyday existence" and "exhort people to pursue causes greater than their personal desires. The opposed orientation, self-indulgent materialism, seeks happiness in the pursuit and consumption of material goods."

Self-sacrificial love was memorably illustrated by four World War II chaplains. In 1943, with Nazi submarines sinking ships faster than the Allied forces could replace them, the troop ship SS *Dorchester* steamed out of New York harbor with 902 men headed for Greenland. Among those leaving anxious families behind were Methodist preacher George Fox, Rabbi Alexander Goode, Catholic priest John Washington, and Reformed Church minister Clark Poling. Some 150 miles from their destination, on a moonless night, U-Boat 456 caught the *Dorchester* in its crosshairs. Within moments of the torpedo's impact, stunned men were pouring out of their bunks as the ship began listing. With power cut off, the ship's radio was useless; its escort vessels, unaware of the unfolding tragedy, pushed on in the darkness. On board, chaos reigned as panicky men came up from the hold without life jackets and leapt into overcrowded lifeboats.

As the four chaplains arrived on the steeply sloping deck, they began guiding the men to their boat stations. They opened a storage locker, distributed life jackets, and coaxed the men over the side. When Petty Officer John Mahoney turned back to retrieve his gloves, Rabbi Goode responded, "Never mind. I have two pairs." Only later did Mahoney realize that the rabbi was not conveniently carrying an extra pair; he was giving up his own.

In the icy, oil-smeared water, Private William Bednar heard the chaplains preaching courage and found the strength to swim to a life raft. Still on board, Grady Clark watched in awe as the chaplains handed out the last life jacket and then, with ultimate selflessness, gave away their own. As Clark slipped into the water, he looked back at an unforgettable sight: the four chaplains were standing, with arms linked, praying in Latin, Hebrew, and English. Other men joined them in a huddle as the *Dorchester* slid beneath the sea. "It was the finest thing I have ever seen or hope to see this side of heaven," said John Ladd, another of the 230 survivors.

Volunteerism. Such heroism makes a powerful but admittedly exceptional anecdote. What about more ordinary religious people? Do they also act altruistically? One answer can be found in national surveys of volunteerism and generosity. In the United States, National Opinion Research Center surveys have revealed a correlation between religiosity and compassion. "Volunteering some time to community service" is said to be a "very important obligation" by 19 percent of those attending religious services less than once a year and by 40 percent of those attending every week or more. In studies of college students and the general public, religiously committed individuals (compared to the religiously uncommitted) have reported volunteering more hours, for example, as relief workers, tutors, and campaigners for social justice. Among the 12 percent of Americans whom Gallup labeled "highly spiritually committed," 46 percent reported presently working among the infirm, the poor, or the elderly—double the 22 percent among those "highly uncommitted." In a follow-up Gallup survey, charitable and social service volunteering was reported by 28 percent of those who rated religion "not very important" in their lives and by 50 percent of those who rated it "very important." And 37 percent of those attending religious services yearly or less but 76 percent of those attending weekly reported thinking at least a "fair amount" about "responsibility to the poor."

Do these religious links with volunteerism extend to other communal organizations? *Bowling Alone* author Robert Putnam analyzed national survey data from twenty-two types of organizations, including hobby clubs, professional associations, self-help groups, and service clubs. "It was membership in religious groups," he reports, "that was most closely associated with other forms of civic involvement, like voting, jury service, community projects, talking with neighbors, and giving to charity." In a forthcoming work, Putnam confirms that actively religious people are more involved in community life, including giving to secular organizations and volunteering (even after controlling for many other factors). "Social involvement in a moral community" helps explain the effect, he tells me. Faith communities offer an alternative to our self-absorbed default setting.

Charitable giving. The jest, "When it comes to giving, some people stop at nothing," is seldom true of church and synagogue members. In a Gallup survey, Americans who said they never attended church or synagogue reported giving away 1.1 percent of their incomes. Weekly attenders were two and a half times as generous. This 24 percent of the population gave 48 percent of all charitable contributions. The other three-quarters of Americans gave the remaining half. Follow-up 1990 and 1992 Gallup surveys and a 2001 INDEPENDENT SECTOR survey confirmed the faith-philanthropy correlation.

Is this generosity focused solely on people's own congregations? To the contrary, reports *The Index of Global Philanthropy,* 2007: "Religious people are more charitable than the non-religious not only in giving to their congregations, but also—regardless of income, region, social class, and other demographic variables—significantly more charitable in their secular donations and informal giving." Indeed, notes Syracuse University researcher Arthur Brooks, people who attend worship weekly or more are "inarguably more charitable in *every measurable way.*"

One analysis by *Fortune* magazine of America's top philanthropists found that most are "religious: Jewish,

Mormon, Protestant, and Catholic. And most attributed their philanthropic urges at least in part to their religious backgrounds." And the seven financially largest publicly supported U.S. philanthropies (YMCA, Red Cross, Catholic Charities, Salvation Army, Goodwill, United Jewish Communities, and Boys and Girls Clubs) have one thing in common: religious motivation was behind their founding.

In recent experiments, University of British Columbia researchers discovered that generosity is increased even by just "priming" (subtly activating in people's minds) the concept of God. Participants

> Religion is the mother of philanthropy.
> —FRANK EMERSON ANDREWS, *ATTITUDES TOWARD GIVING* (1953)

first unscrambled sentences, which for some included the words spirit, divine, God, sacred, and prophet. When then given a choice of how many $1 coins to keep and how many to give to an unseen stranger, those who had been primed with the God concepts were more than doubly generous (average of $4.22 versus $1.84). Apparently the subconsciously activated God concept predisposed charity, even for those who weren't thinking about God during the experiment's next phase. Follow-up experiments in the United States and Belgium confirm the phenomenon: priming religious thoughts activates prosocial behaviors.

Moral behaviors. Other moral behaviors also correlate with religiosity. In a U.S. Values Survey, frequent worship attendance predicted lower scores on a dishonesty scale that assessed self-serving lies, tax cheating, and failing to report damaging a parked car.

An examination of studies of the relationship between religion and delinquency studies found that "most delinquent acts were committed by juveniles who had low levels of religious commitment." To be sure, a study of identical and fraternal twins suggests that the association between religiousness and moral behavior is partly attributable to genetics: heredity has a joint influence on both religiosity and social behavior. But of course, it's not so simple. Many people are good without God, and many believers go to sleep behind bars each night. Yet even when controlling for other factors, such as socioeconomic level, neighborhood, and peer influences, kids who go to church are rarely delinquent.

> I want my attorney, my tailor, my valets, and even my wife to believe in God, and I fancy that then I'll be robbed and cuckolded less often.
>
> —VOLTAIRE, "DIALOGUES BETWEEN A, B, AND C" (1768)

Granted, wrote Gordon Allport, "there are pathogenic strains in some religions, such as excessive terror, superstition, a built-in hostility to science, or a palliative defensiveness. But these pathogenic strains are

not found in the great creeds of the world religions."
To judge faith by what Terry Eagleton called "vulgar
caricatures of religious faith that would make a first-
year theology student wince" is like judging science by
eugenics, nuclear warheads, and chemical pollutants.
Is the pre-Christian classical world to be judged by
its infanticide and human sacrifice in the gladiatorial
arena? Is Darwinism to be judged by the Nazis' social
Darwinism? Is atheism to be judged by the reality that
the worst genocides have mostly come from irreligious
tyrants—the 70 million who died under Chairman
Mao, the 20 million who died under Stalin, or the nearly
2 million people who no longer exist because of Pol
Pot (not to mention those exterminated under Nicolae
Ceauşescu, Kim Jong-il, and others)? Should we ask
whether the atheism of twentieth-century Russia and
China influenced their cultures for better or for worse?
Or should we judge science, religion, and atheism
by their noblest ideals and by their positive as well as
negative impacts? Hitler's Holocaust was rooted in a
eugenics that distorted true science, much as religion-
rationalized Crusades, slavery, and homophobia have
violated Jesus' moral bottom line: love God and love
your neighbor (which, as the Good Samaritan parable
made plain, includes strangers).

We faith-heads are often embarrassed by
people who in religion's name display dogmatism,

superstition, or intolerance. But we ask you to consider our courageous and compassionate saints as well. "It is no accident that the only open challenge to the totalitarian state has come from men of deep religious faith," observed the great journalist Walter Lippmann in *The Good Society*. "For in their faith they are vindicated as immortal souls, and from this enhancement of their dignity they find the reason why they must offer a perpetual challenge to the dominion of men over men." Lippmann may have overlooked people of faith who have condoned inhumanity, as did many German Christians under Hitler. Nevertheless, we recall these profiles in courage:

- The theologian-pastor Dietrich Bonhoeffer enduring two years in a Nazi prison before being executed for his opposition to Hitler.

- The pastors of Le Chambon, France, whose five thousand residents sheltered some five thousand Jews, many of them children brought there for refuge while French collaborators elsewhere were delivering Jews to the Nazis. The people of Le Chambon, mostly descendants of a persecuted Protestant group, had been taught by their pastors to "resist whenever our adversaries will demand of us obedience contrary to the orders of the Gospel." Ordered to reveal the sheltered Jews, the head pastor refused, saying, "I don't know of Jews, I only know of human beings."

• El Salvador's only doctoral-level psychologist, Father Ignacio Martin-Baro, who, after surviving six assassination attempts, continued publishing data exposing Salvadoran poverty and oppression until a military death squad gunned him down along with five fellow Jesuits and two of their helpers.

• The Romanian pastor Laszlo Tokes, who, having protested dictator Nicolae Ceauşescu's brutal oppression, suffered being banned, harassed, beaten, and stabbed. Finally his people formed a protective human chain around his church and parsonage, igniting a revolution that in three days swept the country and toppled Ceauşescu.

Another faith-motivated hero was the serene, unpretentious, soft-spoken Eric Liddell, who, thanks to the Oscar-winning movie *Chariots of Fire* became known to the world as a man who was exceptionally committed to his principles. Rather than run on Sunday, he gave up his chance for a likely Olympic gold medal in the hundred meters, suffered the insult of being called a traitor to his country for doing so, and then astonished everyone by instead running and winning the four-hundred-meter race in world record time.

Although Liddell returned home a national hero, his greater heroism began where the movie ends. Shunning fame, fortune, and the next Olympic Games, he slipped out of the limelight to become a missionary to China, where he taught chemistry and English and later worked in rugged conditions among rural peasant people amid suffering and death triggered by Japan's invasion of China during the late 1930s.

By all accounts, Liddell unfailingly radiated good humor and kindness, and because of his smiling good nature, he was often a peacemaker in times of conflict among the peasants and between them and their invaders. Nor was he one to pass by on the other side of the road when someone was suffering or in need of a daring rescue effort. Shortly before Japan entered World War II, his pregnant wife and two daughters left China for the safety of home, and Liddell stayed behind. In 1943, he was rounded up along with eighteen hundred other foreigners into a Japanese internment camp in the Shantung Province of North China. Langdon Gilkey's book *Shantung Compound: The Story of Men and Women Under Pressure*, recounts the conflicts and selfishness that predominated among this assortment of businesspeople, missionaries, doctors, professors, junkies, and prostitutes, all crammed into a former mission station no longer than two football fields and not as wide. Subjected to privation but not torture, malnutrition but not starvation, the "fundamental bent of the total self in all of us was inward, toward our own welfare," observed Gilkey. "And so immersed were we in it that we hardly seemed able to see this in ourselves."

During his two years in the camp, Eric Liddell emerged as its "most outstanding personality," as another book on the Shantung Compound later described him—the one "with a permanent smile." It was he who organized games and worship, taught science to the children, and cared for people of every sort. One Russian prostitute, for whom he put up some shelves, said he was the only man who did anything for her without wanting to be repaid. Gilkey's stark account of self-righteousness and self-centeredness within the camp is broken by this ray of light:

> It is rare indeed that a person has the good fortune to meet a saint, but he came as close to it as anyone I have ever known. Often in an evening of that last year I . . . would pass the games room and peer in to see what the missionaries had cooking for the teenagers. As often as not Eric . . . would be bent over a chessboard or a model boat, or directing some sort of square dance—absorbed, warm and interested, pouring all of himself into this effort to capture the minds and imaginations of those penned-up youths.

If anyone could have done it, he could. . . . In camp
he was in his middle forties, lithe and springy of step
and, above all, overflowing with good humor and
love of life. He was aided by others, to be sure. But it
was Eric's enthusiasm and charm that carried the day
with the whole effort.

In August 2005, two of the camp's youth returned
to China to speak at the sixtieth anniversary celebration
of the camp's liberation. Mary Taylor Previte recalled that
"we children called [Liddell] Uncle Eric—a hero whose
life and words taught us the love of God every day. He
organized games and races for us children—to keep
hope in our hearts." Stephen Metcalf reminisced that
"Eric gave me two things. His worn out running shoes;
my own shoes had worn out and it was winter," and his
'Baton of forgiveness.' He taught me to love my enemies
(the Japanese) and to pray for them."

In all the accounts I have read, Liddell emerges as
a saint, a man whose life was empowered by the hour
of prayer, Bible reading, and meditation with which he
began each day before the others were awake; a man
who according to his closest comrade was "literally,
God-controlled, in his thought, judgment, actions,
words"; a man who befriended everyone and bridged
the gulf between them and the missionaries; a man

who could be seen carrying coal for an old person; a man who offered to sell his Olympic gold watch to buy more sports gear for the children; a man who, weakened by privation and hunger, began quietly to suffer headaches and discouragement, the early signs of a brain disease that, before many even realized he was seriously ill, took his life just months before the camp's liberation.

Happy Faith-Heads

Mirth and misery, like mischief and morality, are, we can surely agree, exhibited by people of all faiths and none. Still, psychological science helps us sift through two contrasting predictions. Does an active faith breed happiness? ("Joy is the serious business of heaven," offered the believer C. S. Lewis in *Letters to Malcolm*.) Or was the skeptic Sigmund Freud (in *The Future of an Illusion*) closer to the truth in describing religion as an "obsessional neurosis" that breeds sexually repressed, guilt-laden unhappiness? Apparently believing Freud was right, part of Christopher Hitchens' case against religion is his surmise that religious belief does "not make its adherents happy." Contrary to what Hitchens claims, the evidence indicates otherwise, as has become widely acknowledged by researchers. Let's look at some examples.

- The Gallup Organization's 1984 "Religion in America" survey first exposed me to the faith-happiness correlation. Individuals highest in "spiritual commitment" (those who consistently agreed with statements such as "God loves me even though I may not always please him" and "My religious faith is the most important influence in my life") were twice as likely as those least spiritually committed to report being "very happy."

• National Opinion Research Center surveys from 1972 to the present reveal higher self-reported happiness among Americans who feel "extremely close to God" (40 percent "very happy") rather than "not very close" (21 percent) or "not close at all" (24 percent). (There are no marked differences by religion; about one in three Protestants, Catholics, and Jews have reported themselves very happy.)

• These surveys also reveal a marked correlation between frequency of religious attendance and self-reported happiness (see Figure 7). A comparable result was obtained by a recent Pew study of American happiness: 43 percent of frequent (weekly or more) attenders but only 26 percent of seldom or never attenders reporting themselves "very happy."

• When the Gallup Organization extended this association to life satisfaction, 55 percent of "engaged" congregational members reported being "completely satisfied with the conditions of my life," while just

FIGURE 7. Percentage of People Reporting Themselves "Very Happy,"
by Religious Attendance, 1972–2004.

Source: National Opinion Research Center.

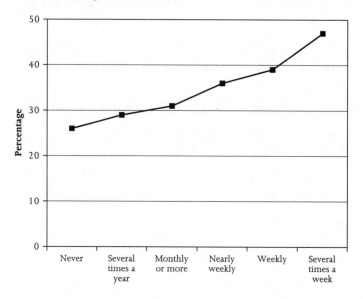

25 percent of those "actively disengaged" reported that level of satisfaction.

• A statistical digest of the slew of 1980s studies focused on the association between religiousness and well-being among the elderly found that the two best predictors of well-being among older persons were health and religiousness. Elderly people tend to be happier and more satisfied with life if religiously committed and engaged.

- Karl Marx believed that "the abolition of religion as the illusory happiness of the people is required for their real happiness." Karl Marx was wrong.

Other studies have explored the connection between religious faith and coping with crises and loss. Compared to religiously inactive new widows, recently widowed women who worship regularly have reported more joy in their lives. Among mothers of developmentally challenged children, those with a deep religious faith are less vulnerable to depression. People of faith also tend to retain or recover greater happiness after suffering divorce, unemployment, serious illness, or bereavement. Not surprisingly, then, a 2003 statistical digest of more than two hundred studies revealed that high religiousness predicts a mildly lower risk of depression, especially for individuals undergoing stress. A follow-up study of thirty-seven thousand Canadians reported that "higher worship frequency was associated with lower odds of psychiatric disorders." Actively religious North Americans have also been much less likely than the irreligious to become delinquent, to abuse drugs and alcohol, and to commit suicide.

Why does faith seem to have such a positive effect? An active religious faith hardly precludes stress or suffering (as the biblical story of Job reminds people of the Abrahamic faiths). Yet religiousness correlates with

expressed happiness and helps buffer stress. Seeking to
explain the correlation, researchers have entertained
several possibilities.

Social support: "*Where two or three are gathered.*" If Martin
Seligman is right that "rampant individualism" has
contributed to today's elevated depression rates, and if
humans indeed have a fundamental "need to belong,"
then one factor is surely the social support provided by
North America's estimated 350,000 faith communities.
People usually practice their religion communally,
through "the fellowship of kindred spirits," "the bearing
of one another's burdens," "the ties of love that bind."
As John Winthrop explained to one of the first groups of
Puritans before disembarking to their new world, "We
must delight in each other, make others' conditions our
own, rejoice together, mourn together, labor and suffer
together, always having before our eyes our community
as members of the same body." Pennsylvania's
communal old-order Amish are known not only for
their agrarian, pacifistic culture but also for their low
rates of major depression.

Meaning and purpose: "*Something worth living and dying for.*"
The social benefit of faith communities matters, but it's
not all that matters. After controlling for (extracting the
effect of) the greater support experienced by actively
religious folk, some correlation between religiousness
and well-being remains. The nineteenth-century Polish

poet Cyprian Norwid offered a clue to another possible factor: "To be what is called happy, one should have (1) something to live on, (2) something to live for, (3) something to die for. The lack of one of these results in drama. The lack of two results in tragedy."

Studies confirm that a sense of life's meaning and purpose enhances well-being and that many people find such through their religious faith. Martin Seligman has argued that a loss of meaning is another reason for today's high depression rate and that finding meaning requires "an attachment to something larger than the lonely self. To the extent that young people now find it hard to take seriously their relationship with God, to care about their relationship with the country or to be part of a large and abiding family, they will find it very difficult to find meaning in life. To put it another way, the self is a very poor site for finding meaning." Harvesting data from the National Longitudinal Survey of Freshmen, sociologist Margarita Mooney found that even after controlling for other factors known to predict achievement, religiously active students studied more, got better grades, and were more satisfied with their college experience. Religion, she reports, "provides a work ethic or sense of meaning in college."

In the Nazi death camps, Viktor Frankl similarly observed a lowered apathy and death rate among fellow inmates who retained a sense of meaning, a purpose for which to live or even be willing to die for. Many of these, he reported, were devout Jews, who found in their faith the strength to live and to resist their oppressors.

> [Religion satisfies] the most fundamental human need of all. That is the need to know that somehow we matter, that our lives mean something, count as something more than just a momentary blip in the universe.
>
> —RABBI HAROLD KUSHNER, "MY RELIGIOUS FAITH" (1987)

Durable self-esteem: "Accepting God's love." Although self-esteem has been overplayed in today's pop psychology, it does predict happiness. Paul Tillich and other theologians have argued that the religious message that God loves you—just as you are—can form a psychological basis for a secure and durable self-worth. No longer is there any need to define one's self-worth by achievements, material well-being, or social approval. To find self-acceptance, said Tillich, "do not seek for anything; do not perform anything; do not intend anything. *Simply accept the fact that you are accepted!* . . . If that happens to us, we experience grace. After such an experience we may not be better than before, and we may not believe more than before. But everything is transformed."

People who have this idea of God's "grace"—who see God as redemptively loving, accepting, and caring—enjoy not only greater self-esteem but also warmer marriages, reported the survey researcher Andrew Greeley.

There is a seeming interplay between our God concept and our self-concept.

Terror management: An "eternal perspective." Writing from a college whose symbol is the "Anchor of Hope," I cannot resist noting what my late psychologist colleague C. R. Snyder so often reminded us of: the psychological significance of hope. Many religious worldviews do more than propose answers to some of life's deepest questions; they also encourage an ultimate hope, especially when

> Hope is itself a species of happiness, and, perhaps, the chief happiness which this world affords.
>
> —SAMUEL JOHNSON, IN BOSWELL'S *LIFE OF SAMUEL JOHNSON* (1791)

confronting what the psychologists Sheldon Solomon, Jeffery Greenberg, and Tom Pyszczynski call "the terror resulting from our awareness of vulnerability and death." Christianity struggles with the problem of evil (If God is both all-powerful and all good, why do bad things happen?). But at least it acknowledges rather than denies evil, as Richard Dawkins does in arguing that the universe has "no evil and no good, nothing but blind pitiless indifference." Try explaining that devaluing of life and of loss to someone who has just suffered the death of a child and who may also believe the Christian message that God, who has identified with human suffering, suffers with us and ultimately will redeem the situation.

Different faiths offer different paths, but most offer its adherents a sense that they, or something meaningful they are part of, will survive their death. Aware of the great enemies, suffering and death, they offer a hope that in the end, the very end, "all shall be well and all shall be well and all manner of things shall be well" (as the fourteenth-century Christian mystic Julian of Norwich famously said). That hope may help people cope with whatever punctuates life between now and death. Or so it seems from a recent national study of adult Americans that found that "belief in life after death was consistently and directly related to better mental health after controlling for other variables."

The scientist David Sloan Wilson, though a nonbeliever, sees biological (group-survival-promoting) wisdom underlying religion. Working with samplings of people's experience from the psychologist Mihaly Csikszentmihalyi's studies, he also reports that "religious believers are more prosocial than non-believers, feel better about themselves, use their time more constructively, and engage in long-term planning rather than gratifying their impulsive desires. On a moment-by-moment basis, they report being more happy, active, sociable, involved and excited." His conclusion: "Dawkins' diatribe against religion, however well-intentioned, is . . . deeply misinformed."

Healthy Faith-Heads

As humans have suffered ills and sought healing throughout history, religion and medicine have joined hands in caring for them. Often those hands belonged to the same person; the spiritual leader was also the healer. Maimonides was a twelfth-century rabbi and a renowned physician. Michael Servetus, the sixteenth-century physician who first described the pulmonary circulation, was also a Spanish theologian. Hospitals, which were first established in monasteries and then spread by missionaries, often carry the names of saints or faith communities.

As medical science matured, healing and religion diverged. Rather than asking God to spare their children from smallpox, people were able to vaccinate them. Rather than seeking a spiritual healer when burning with bacterial fever, they were able to use antibiotics. Recently, however, as research has explored patients' spiritual needs and how faith supports coping, religion and healing have been converging once again:

- Of America's 135 medical schools, 101 offered spirituality and health courses in 2005, up from 5 in 1992.

- Duke University has established the Center for Spirituality, Theology, and Health.

- A Yankelovich survey found that 94 percent of U.S. HMO professionals and 99 percent of family physicians agreed that "personal prayer, meditation, or other spiritual and religious practices" can enhance medical treatment.

- A National Library of Medicine MEDLINE search of "religion" or "spirituality" reveals 8,719 articles between 2000 and 2007, four and a half times the 1,950 articles in all the database's prior years, 1965 to 1999.

Is there fire underneath all this smoke? More than a thousand studies have sought to correlate the "faith factor" with health and healing. As the author of an introductory psychology text that includes a chapter on health psychology, I once sympathized with the skeptics; I wasn't convinced and so didn't present the religion-health research. Gradually, however, I became persuaded that despite disagreements over their interpretation, the new epidemiological studies merited reporting.

For example, Jeremy Kark and his colleagues compared the death rates for 3,900 Israelis either in one of eleven religiously Orthodox or in one of eleven matched, nonreligious collective settlements (kibbutz communities). The researchers reported that over a sixteen-year period, "belonging to a religious collective was associated with a strong protective effect" not explained by age or economic differences. In every age group, religious community members were about half as likely to have died as their nonreligious counterparts. This is roughly comparable to the differing death rates of men and women in the same age group.

In response to such findings, Richard Sloan, in various articles and in *Blind Faith: The Unholy Alliance of Religion and Medicine*, articulates a skepticism you may share, partly by reminding us that mere correlations can leave many factors uncontrolled. Consider one obvious possibility: women are more religiously active than men, and women outlive men. So perhaps religious involvement is merely an expression of the gender effect on longevity.

However, several new studies find the religiosity-longevity correlation among men alone and even more strongly among women. One study that followed 5,286 Californians over twenty-eight years found that after controlling for gender (as well as age, ethnicity, and education), frequent religious attendees were 36 percent less likely to have died in any year.

A U.S. National Health Interview Survey followed 21,204 people over eight years. After controlling for age, sex, race, and region, researchers found that those who did not attend religious services were 1.87 times more likely to have died than those who attended more than weekly. This translated into a life expectancy at age twenty of seventy-five years for infrequent attenders and eighty-three years for frequent attenders. This correlational finding does not indicate that nonattenders who start attending services and change nothing else will live eight years longer. But it does indicate that as a *predictor* of health and longevity, religious involvement rivals nonsmoking and exercise.

How to explain such findings? First, religiously active people have healthier lifestyles; for example, they smoke and drink less. Health-oriented, vegetarian Seventh-Day Adventists have a longer-than-usual life expectancy. Religiously Orthodox Israelis eat less fat than their nonreligious compatriots. But such differences are not great enough to explain the dramatically reduced mortality in the religious kibbutzim, argued the Israeli researchers. In the recent American studies, too, about 75 percent of the longevity difference remains after controlling for unhealthy behaviors such as inactivity and smoking.

For health, as for happiness, social support also matters. Moreover, religion encourages another predictor of health and longevity: marriage. In the religious kibbutzim, for example, divorce has been almost nonexistent. In the United States too, people of active faith have low divorce rates.

But even after controlling for gender, unhealthy behaviors, social ties, and preexisting health problems, the mortality studies find much of the mortality reduction remaining. Researchers speculate that this may be so because of several additional variables: the stress protection and enhanced well-being associated with a coherent worldview, a sense of hope for the long-term future, feelings of ultimate acceptance, and the relaxed meditation of prayer or Sabbath observance. These variables might also help explain other recent findings among the religiously active, such as healthier immune functioning and fewer hospital admissions and, for AIDS patients, fewer stress hormones and longer survival.

Does Explaining Religion Explain It Away?

I hope that it is by now clear, my skeptic friends, that my response to those who view religion as "both false and dangerous" is this: there exists a faith perspective that is both rationally plausible and conducive to human flourishing. Moreover, when people ask me, "How can you, as a Christian, embrace evolution? Advocate gay marriage? Agree with the prayer experiment skeptics? Report so enthusiastically on psychological science?" my response is that I embrace science and draw these conclusions not *despite* my faith but motivated and set free by my faith.

Still, you may wonder, can't we deconstruct the "religion factor" that predicts happiness and health into its psychological components? Religion, we've noted, encompasses social support, a purpose for living, devotion to a reality beyond self, a basis for self-acceptance, hope for the timeless future, and the promotion of positive character traits. If we were to control for all such ingredients, would there be

anything left of the religion factor? But that would
be like a hurricane analyst wondering whether after
controlling for the effects of the wind, rain, and tidal
surge, there remains any intrinsic effect of a hurricane.
Both hurricanes and religion are package variables.
Religion, for example, almost by definition entails
social support. The Latin root of religion, *religio*,
means "to bind together." Unlike individualistic forms
of New Age spirituality, religious communities are
intrinsically communal.

But don't psychological explanations of
religion, from Freud's wish fulfillment to today's
evolutionary psychology, diminish its credibility? Wasn't
sociobiologist E. O. Wilson right to propose that "we
have come to the crucial stage in the history of biology
when religion itself is subject to the explanations of the
natural sciences. . . . Theology is not likely to survive as
an independent intellectual discipline." One can indeed
understand religion as adaptive and beneficial, as David
Sloan Wilson does in *Darwin's Cathedral*, while still viewing
it as irrational.

And one can also understand that neuroscientists
might find brain "hot spots" during spiritual states
without presuming that this is a created "space for God."
Given that everything psychological is simultaneously
biological, the discovery of brain activity associated with
spirituality is unsurprising. It neither proves God ("Why

would there be a space for God if there were no God?")
nor disproves God ("Spirituality has been reduced to
mere brain activity").

The point to remember is this: *explaining a belief
does not explain it away.* The truth of a belief is logically
distinct from its psychological function. Imagine that
E. O. Wilson, David Sloan Wilson, and their kindred
spirits (such as Michael Shermer, author of *How We
Believe*) complete their work, with a full and finished
evolutionary psychology of religion. Imagine that
simultaneously, other researchers who are studying
the "psychology of unbelief" (an actual book title
from some years ago) arrive at a full understanding
of atheism. (Might atheism be adaptive because it
reduces restraints on sexual reproduction and nullifies
religion's teachings regarding the claims of the poor
on our material resources? "If God does not exist, the
seven deadly sins are not terrors to be overcome but
temptations to be enjoyed," notes Dinesh D'Souza, in
offering one psychological explanation for the appeal
of atheism.) We could even imagine a day when,
paraphrasing E. O. Wilson, someone might say that
atheism itself has become subject to the explanations of
the natural sciences and is therefore not likely to survive
as a credible idea.

But here we must rise to the defense of atheism
as well as theism. If both belief systems come to be

explained, as would happen if psychological science completes its work, that cannot mean they both are false. You and I can surely agree that either God exists or does not, so one of these beliefs must be true.

The point can be extended to any other belief or attitude. Knowing why you believe something needn't say anything about its truth or falsity. Thus the Oxford University psychologist Justin Barrett, a Christian, can comfortably study religion as a natural product of our mental architecture. Scientifically explaining mental phenomena needn't mean we should stop believing them, he notes. "Suppose science produces a convincing account for why I think my wife loves me— should I then stop believing that she does?" Likewise, scientifically explaining why one person believes vegetarianism is healthiest and another believes that meat eating is healthiest does not decide which is right. As Keith Ward has noted, Francis Crick's contention in *The Astonishing Hypothesis*—that you "are in fact no more than the behavior of a vast assembly of nerve cells and their associated molecules"—can as well be said of your belief that 2 plus 2 equals 4.

So, I have advised students, let no one say to you, and never say to anyone, "Your beliefs can be dismissed because you only believe them for such and such reasons." Archbishop William Temple recognized the distinction between explaining and explaining away when he was challenged after an Oxford address: "Well, of course, Archbishop, the point is that you believe what you believe because of the way you were brought up." To which the archbishop replied, "That is as it may be. But the fact remains that you believe that I believe what I believe because of the way I was brought up, because of the way you were brought up."

Moreover, does the scientific account of religion's functionality diminish religion? Or would it be a greater embarrassment to religion if Freud and the evolutionary psychologists were proved wrong—if religion were found to serve no useful psychological purpose? If, as we people of faith believe, God loves us, then should we be surprised that genuine worship and belief has some secondary benefits?

The point can be extended to moral ideas. Despite cultural variations, some moral ideas exist across cultures and faiths. In *The Abolition of Man*, C. S. Lewis called these universal moral teachings the "natural law" or "Tao." An illustration came from the 1993 World Parliament of Religion: "Every form of egoism should be rejected. . . . We must treat others as we wish others to treat us. . . . We consider humankind our family." Evolutionary psychologists agree that some universal moral laws exist and offer explanations of "how nature designed our universal sense of right and wrong" (the subtitle of Marc Hauser's *Moral Minds*). Indeed, elements of morality can be found in the empathy, sympathy, and communalism of primates, which can be explained by our genetic predisposition to further our genes, both through mutually supportive actions (reciprocity) and by helping others with whom we share genes (kin selection). Francis Collins agrees that moral ideas are encoded in the human genome, though to him such ideas are "the language of God." God works through, not apart from, created nature.

Theism does, however, have implications for our sense of moral urgency. Much as an explanation of one person's theism and another's atheism does not decide God's existence, so an explanation of morality gives no compelling rationale for how we should act when no one is watching. A powerful idea—that all people are God's children whom the creator admonishes us to love—beckons us to a selflessness that atheistic materialism does not. It gives my friends Judy and Dennis a reason to spend time building latrines outside Ethiopian village schools. It gives my daughter, Laura, a reason to spend the best years of her life mentoring youth from Cape Town's townships. And it gives us a reason to consider ourselves as stewards rather than possessors of any wealth placed in our care.

Gregg Easterbrook laments Richard Dawkins' idea that in a universe of "blind physical forces and genetic replication, some people are going to get hurt, others are going to get lucky, and you won't find any rhyme or reason for it." "How convenient," Easterbrook responded, "that someone who has himself won a privileged position in life blames only a callous universe—not lack of action by persons in privileged positions—for the needs of the less fortunate. If there is higher purpose, then we have obligations to one another and will be judged if those obligations go unmet."

Shortly after writing the preceding paragraph, I was invited to a preview showing of *Sold: Fighting the New Global Slave Trade*, featuring three contemporary abolitionists: an African Christian dedicated to reversing Togo's child labor trafficking, a Hindu doctor who rescues women and children from India's brothels, and a Muslim attorney who has pressured the United Arab Emirates to stop exploiting and harming young Pakistani and Bangladeshi boys as camel jockeys. Each is said to be "motivated by the potent idea that every human is created in the image of a divine creator and that each of us will ultimately be held accountable for what we have done to alleviate the suffering of others." If only Stalin, Mao, and Pol Pot would have had the same idea.

The Leap of Faith

So at the end of the day, we are each free to choose. We can view the longing for God as a God-shaped vacuum meant to be fulfilled, much as a baby's hunger foretells the reality of food (as C. S. Lewis suggested). Or we can view the human yen to perceive an invisible agency as an adaptive illusion.

If religion is, on balance, adaptive rather than toxic—if it bends us toward happiness, health, and helpfulness—that is worth knowing. But it still leaves truth up for grabs. And truth is what matters. If religious claims were shown to be untrue, though comforting and adaptive, what honest person would choose to believe? And if religious claims were shown to be true, though discomfiting, what honest person would choose to disbelieve?

So what is the truth? The new atheists dismiss various "proofs" for God and expose what seems bad in the early part of the "Good Book." "The God of the Old Testament," says Dawkins in The God Delusion's most pungent sentence, "is arguably the most unpleasant character in all fiction: jealous and proud of it; a petty, unjust, unforgiving control freak; a vindictive, bloodthirsty ethnic cleanser; a misogynist, homophobic, racist, infanticidal, genocidal, filicidal, pestilential, megalomaniacal, sadomasochistic, capriciously malevolent bully."

Bum rap, respond the biblical scholars and theologians. The multifaceted biblical material offers characterizations of God that contradict each of these aspersions. Moreover, Scripture offers an unfolding revelation of God, who comes to be understood as benevolent and loving.

Taking time out from this slugfest, can we admit to one another that each of us feels at least a dash of agnosticism, of uncertainty, about our own theism or atheism? In the dark of night, have we not each had moments when we have wondered whether the other is right? Perhaps there is, as Richard Dawkins assumes, no God, no purpose, "nothing but blind pitiless indifference." Perhaps "God" is just a word we use to cover our ignorance. Perhaps all spiritual intuitions are illusions.

Or perhaps Albert Einstein was right to chide "fanatical atheists" as "creatures who—in their grudge against traditional religion as the 'opiate of the masses'— cannot hear the music of the spheres." Perhaps it is human ignorance to presume God's absence from the fabric of the universe. Perhaps those who miss a spiritual dimension

> Sometimes I think we're alone. Sometimes I think we're not. In either case, the thought is staggering.
>
> —ATTRIBUTED TO R. BUCKMINSTER FULLER

are flatlanders who miss the nonmaterial reality.

When reason cannot decide, we justifiably listen to our hearts, argued William James: "Our passional nature" must decide between genuine, important options that cannot "be decided on intellectual grounds." For James, to yield to our hope that "the religious hypothesis" may be true, and to live accordingly, was wiser than to yield to our fear of its "being error." "If religion be true and the evidence for it be still insufficient, I do not wish, by putting your extinguisher upon my nature . . . to forfeit my sole chance in life of getting upon the winning side—that chance depending, of course, on my willingness to run the risk of acting as if my passional need of taking the world religiously might be prophetic and right."

Or, lacking certainty, should we straddle the fence with perfect indecision? That's the advice of some, notes James: "Keep your mind in suspense forever, rather than [incurring] the awful risk of believing lies. . . . To preach skepticism to us as a duty until 'sufficient evidence' for religion be found, is tantamount therefore to telling us, when in the presence of the religious hypothesis, that to yield to our fear of its being error is wiser and better than to yield to our hope that it may be true." But sometimes, Albert Camus reportedly said, life beckons us to make a 100 percent commitment to something about which we are 51 percent sure.

Credit Richard Dawkins, Sam Harris, Christopher Hitchens, and the other uncompromising atheists for the courage to leap off the fence and stir the debate. The success of science and the lack of direct evidence of divine activity, combined with the superstitions and inhumanity sometimes practiced in religion's name, understandably push some people to take a leap of faith to the skeptical side of the fence. If David Hume was right to believe that "truth springs from argument among friends," then all of us who are truth seekers should welcome the robust argument over whether religion is "false and dangerous."

But may we also then credit people of faith, especially those who embody faith-rooted empiricism, for venturing a leap of faith? Existence is a mystery, a mystery embraced in the journey of faith. For Christians, the poetic opening words of the Gospel of John express the mystery: "In the beginning was the Word, and the Word was with God, and the Word was God. . . . And the Word became flesh and lived among us." "Faith is taking the first step even when you don't see the whole staircase," said Martin Luther King Jr. Many people have ventured that first step mindful that they might be wrong yet willing to bet their lives on a humble spirituality, on a third alternative to purposeless scientism and dogmatic fundamentalism. Such spirituality, rooted in the developing biblical wisdom and in a faith tradition that crosses the centuries, helps make sense of the universe, gives meaning to life, opens us to the transcendent, connects us in supportive communities, provides a mandate for morality and selflessness, and offers hope in the face of adversity and death.

Surely, in some ways I'm wrong, you're wrong, we're all wrong. We glimpse ultimate reality as in a dim mirror, constrained by our cognitive limits. Perhaps, then, we can draw wisdom from both skepticism and spirituality by anchoring our lives in a rationality and humility that restrains spirituality with critical analysis and in a spirituality that nurtures purpose, love, joy, and hope.

Appendix
International Society for Science and Religion Statement on Intelligent Design

The International Society for Science and Religion is a scholarly society devoted to ongoing dialogue between the sciences and the community of world faiths (see issr.org.uk). It was established in 2002 for the purpose of promoting education through the support of

Note: This statement was written by Denis Alexander of Cambridge University; Munawar A. Anees, founding editor of *Periodica Islamica*; Martinez Hewlett of the University of Arizona; Ronald L. Numbers (chair) of the University of Wisconsin; Holmes Rolston III of Colorado State University; Michael Ruse of Florida State University; and Jeffery A. Schloss of Westmont College. The authors constitute a group set up for the purpose by the Executive Committee of the International Society for Science and Religion. Through a process involving consultation with all members of the Society, the statement was accepted in February 2008 by the Executive Committee for publication as a statement made on behalf of the Society. The Society retains the copyright of the statement but gives general permission to reproduce it, in whole or in part, provided that this explanation is reproduced.

interdisciplinary learning and research in the fields of science and religion, conducted where possible in an international and multi-faith context.

The society greatly values modern science, while deploring efforts to drive a wedge between science and religion. Science operates with a common set of methodological approaches that gives freedom to scientists from a range of religious backgrounds to unite in a common endeavor. This approach does not deny the existence of a metaphysical realm but rather opens up the natural world to a range of explorations that have been incredibly productive, especially over the last 400 years or so.

The intelligent-design (ID) movement began in the late 1980s as a challenge to the perceived secularization of the scientific community, which leaders of the movement maintained had been coloured with the philosophy of atheistic naturalism. ID theorists have focused their critique primarily on biological evolution and the neo-Darwinian paradigm. They claim that because certain biological features appear to be "irreducibly complex" and thus incapable of evolving incrementally by natural selection, they must have been created by the intervention of an intelligent designer. Despite this focus on evolution, intelligent design should not be confused with biblical or "scientific" creationism, which relies on a particular interpretation of the Genesis account of creation.

We believe that intelligent design is neither sound science nor good theology. Although the boundaries of science are open to change, allowing supernatural explanations to count as science undercuts the very purpose of science, which is to explain the workings of nature without recourse to religious language. Attributing complexity to the interruption of natural law by a divine designer is, as some critics have claimed, a science stopper. Besides, ID has not yet opened up a new research program. In the opinion of the overwhelming majority of research biologists, it has not provided examples of "irreducible complexity" in biological evolution that could not be explained as well by normal scientifically understood processes. Students of nature once considered the vertebrate eye to be too complex to explain naturally, but subsequent research has led to the conclusion that this remarkable structure can be readily understood as a product of natural selection. This shows that what may appear to be "irreducibly complex" today may be explained naturalistically tomorrow.

Scientific explanations are always incomplete. We grant that a comprehensive account of evolutionary natural history remains open to complementary philosophical, metaphysical, and religious dimensions. Darwinian natural history does preempt certain accounts of creation, leading, for example, to the contemporary creationist and ID controversies. However, in most instances, biology and religion operate at different and non-competing levels. In many religious traditions, such as some found in Hinduism, Buddhism, and Taoism, the notion of intelligent design is irrelevant. We recognize that natural theology may be a legitimate enterprise in its own right, but we resist the insistence of intelligent-design advocates that their enterprise be taken as genuine science—just as we oppose efforts of others to elevate science into a comprehensive world view (so-called scientism).

Notes

False and Dangerous?

p. 1   *"sanctimoniously hypocritical"*: Richard Dawkins, *The God Delusion* (Boston: Houghton Mifflin, 2006), p. 292.

p. 1   *"nod maniacally . . ."*: Ibid., p. 166.

p. 2   *"both false and dangerous"*: Sam Harris, *Letter to a Christian Nation* (New York: Knopf, 2006), p. 47.

p. 2   *"violent, irrational, . . ."*: Christopher Hitchens, *God Is Not Great: How Religion Poisons Everything* (New York: Twelve, 2007), p. 56.

p. 2   *religion's golden calves*: Ralph Skinner, "Why Christians Should Take Richard Dawkins Seriously," *Ekklesia*, Sept. 28, 2007 [ekklesia.co.uk].

My Assumptions

p. 5   *short list of ultimate questions*: Leo Tolstoy, *My Confessions* (Boston: Dana Estes, 1904).

p. 6   *Moses*: Deuteronomy 18:22 (Today's English Version).

p. 6   *Gamaliel*: Acts 5:38–39 (New Revised Standard Version).

p. 6   *Saint Paul*: Thessalonians 5:22.

p. 6   *eighth edition*: David G. Myers, *Psychology*, 8th ed. (New York: Worth, 2006).

p. 6   *intuition*: David G. Myers, *Intuition: Its Powers and Perils* (New Haven, Conn.: Yale University Press, 2002).

Mea Culpa

p. 9   *"There exist pathologies . . ."*: Pope Benedict XVI, cited by Russell
        Shorto, "Keeping the Faith," *New York Times Magazine*, Apr. 2007
        [nytimes.com].

The Dance of Fanatics and Infidels

p. 11   *attacking God; teaching children faith*: Dawkins, *God Delusion*,
        pp. 307–308.
p. 12   *"Never pit science against religion"*: Alan I. Leshner, "Science and
        Public Engagement," *Chronicle of Higher Education*, Oct. 13, 2006,
        p. B20.
p. 12   *"fight against intelligent design"*: Michael Ruse, "Fighting the
        Fundamentalists: Chamberlain or Churchill?" *Skeptical Inquirer*,
        2007, 31, 38.
p. 12   *"Darwinism equals atheism"*: Ibid., 41.
p. 12   *Johnson's challenge to evolutionary theory*: "Doubting Rationalist:
        'Intelligent Design' Proponent Phillip Johnson and How He
        Came to Be," *Washington Post*, May 15, 2005, p. D1.
p. 13   *"deranged, deluded, . . ."*: Alister McGrath, *The Dawkins Delusion? Atheist
        Fundamentalism and the Denial of the Divine* (Nottingham, England:
        IVP Books, 2007).
p. 13   *"no design, no purpose, . . ."*: Richard Dawkins, *River out of Eden: A
        Darwinian View of Life* (London: Phoenix, 1995), p. 133.
p. 13   *"Fanatics and infidels . . ."*: Richard Schweder, "Atheists Agonistes,"
        New York Times, Nov. 27, 2006 [nytimes.com].

Simplistic Stereotypes

p. 15   *Keith Ward*: Personal communication (review of *The God Delusion*),
        Mar. 6, 2007.
p. 15   *lumping all religions together*: Harris, *Letter to a Christian Nation*, p. 47;
        Richard Dawkins, "Is Science a Religion?" *Humanist*, Jan.-Feb.
        1997 [thehumanist.org/humanist/articles/dawkins.html].
p. 15   *"religions are diverse . . ."*: David Sloan Wilson, "Beyond
        Demonic Memes: Why Richard Dawkins Is Wrong

About Religion," *eSkeptic*, July 4, 2007 [skeptic.com/skeptic/07-07-04.html].

The Heart of Science and Religion

p. 17   *"Judeo-Christian philosophical framework"*: Owen Gingerich, *God's Universe* (Cambridge, Mass.: Harvard University Press, 2006), p. 6.

p. 18   *Psalms*: Psalm 19:1 (New Revised Standard Version).

p. 18   *Saint Paul*: Romans 1:20a (New Revised Standard Version).

p. 18   *"I am free . . ."*: Nathanael Carpenter, *Philosophia Libera* (Oxford: Lichfield & Short, 1622).

p. 18   *Saint Paul*: 2 Timothy 4:3–4 (New Revised Standard Version).

p. 20   *finding God's path in physical laws*: James E. Bultman, "Presidential Update, Fall 2005," Fall 2005 [hope.edu/admin/president/presupdf2005.html].

p. 21   *"'tell it like it is'"*: Donald MacKay, "Letters," *Journal of the American Scientific Affiliation*, Dec. 1984, p. 237.

p. 21   *as Jesus intimated*: John 16:12–13 NRSV.

The Skeptics' Boys Club

p. 22   *list of rationalist skeptics*: Deborah Frisch, "Skeptical of Skepticism," *Skeptical Inquirer*, May–June 2000, pp. 59–60.

p. 22   *Skeptics Society survey*: Michael Shermer, *How We Believe: The Search for God in an Age of Science* (New York: Freeman, 1999).

p. 24   *Damasio experiments*: Antoine Bechara, Hanna Damasio, Daniel Tranel, and Antonio R. Damasio, "Deciding Advantageously Before Knowing the Advantageous Strategy," *Science*, 1997, *275*, 1293–1297.

p. 25   *"I have no basis whatever . . ."*: Martin Gardner, "Faith: Why I Am Not an Atheist," in *The Whys of a Philosophical Scrivener* (New York: St. Martin's Press, 1999), p. 222.

Inseparable Body and Soul

p. 27   *"lodged in my body"*: René Descartes: *The Meditations and Selections from the Principles of René Descartes* (LaSalle, Ill.: Open Court Publishing, 1948), p. 94.

p. 27   *"Everything in science to date ..."*: Roger Sperry, "Changed Concepts of Brain and Consciousness: Some Value Implications," *Zygon*, 1985, *20*, 41–57.

p. 29   *near-death experiences*: Ronald Siegel, "Of the Brain: The Psychology of Life After Death," *American Psychologist*, 1980, *35*, 911–931.

p. 31   *"If the Psychical Researchers ..."*: C. S. Lewis, *Miracles* (San Francisco: HarperOne, 2001), p. 238.

Does Prayer "Work"?

p. 34   *"do not heap up empty phrases"*: Matthew 6:7 (New Revised Standard Version).

p. 36   *my notarized statement*: David G. Myers, "Why People of Faith Can Expect Null Effects in the Harvard Prayer Experiment," 1997 [davidmyers.org/davidmyers/assets/prayer -letter.pdf].

p. 39   *experiments as blasphemy*: Keith Stewart Thompson, "The Revival of Experiments on Prayer," *American Scientist*, Nov.-Dec. 1996, pp. 532–534.

p. 39   *"impossibility of empirical proof"*: C. S. Lewis, *Miracles* (New York: Macmillan, 1947), p. 215.

p. 40   *other prayer experiments*: For a comprehensive statistical synopsis of intercessory prayer experiments—revealing "no discernible effects"—see Kevin S. Masters and Glen I. Spielmans, "Prayer and Health: Review, Meta-Analysis, and Research Agenda," *Journal of Behavioral Medicine*, 2007, *30*, 329–338.

p. 41   *in vitro fertilization experiment*: Bruce Flamm, "Third Strike for Columbia University Prayer Study: Author Plagiarism," *Skeptical Inquirer*, May-June 2007, pp. 19–20.

p. 42   *kingdom of God*: Luke 17:21 (Revised Standard Version).

The Benevolent, Fine-Tuned Universe

p. 45   Nature *editorial*: "Evolution and the Brain," *Nature*, 2007, 447, 753.

p. 45   *single best idea*: Daniel C. Dennett, *Darwin's Dangerous Idea: Evolution and the Meanings of Life* (New York: Simon & Schuster, 1995), p. 21.

p. 46   *exactly what Darwin predicts*: Francis Collins, *The Language of God* (New York: Free Press, 2006), p. 130.

p. 46   *Saint Augustine*: Quoted by John Noble Wilford in "New Findings Help Balance the Cosmological Books," *New York Times*, Feb. 9, 1999 [nytimes.com].

p. 46   *Warfield*: Benjamin B. Warfield, "On the Antiquity and the Unity of the Human Race," *Princeton Theological Review*, 1911, *9*, 1–26.

p. 47   *science-religion dialogue*: John Paul II, "Truth Cannot Contradict Truth," address to the Pontifical Academy of Sciences, Oct. 22, 1996.

p. 47   *Nowak*: Martin Nowak, "Evolution and Christianity," lecture given at the Harvard Divinity School, Mar. 2007.

p. 47   *"The evidence for evolution . . ."*: National Academy of Sciences, *Science, Evolution, and Creationism* (Washington, D.C.: National Academies Press, 2008), quoted in a National Academies press release, Jan. 3, 2008.

p. 48   *Gallup poll*: Frank Newport, "Majority of Republicans Doubt Theory of Evolution: More Americans Accept Theory of Creationism Than Evolution," June 11, 2007 [galluppoll.com].

p. 48   *Newsweek survey*: "Newsweek Poll: 90% Believe in God," *Newsweek*, Mar. 30, 2007 [msnbc.msn.com].

p. 48   *criticism of creationists*: Collins, *Language of God*, p. 177.

p. 48   *intelligent design*: Ibid., p. 195.

p. 50   *"Now we see . . ."*: Robert Jastrow, *God and the Astronomers* (New York: Norton, 1992), p. 14.

p. 50   *Penzias*: Quoted in Malcolm Browne, "Clues to the Universe's Origin Expected," *New York Times*, Mar. 12, 1978, p. 1.

p. 51   *coin toss*: Paul Davies, *The Cosmic Jackpot: Why Our Universe Is Just Right for Life* (New York: Houghton-Mifflin, 2007), p. 150.

p. 51   *"I can recall vividly . . ."*: Gingerich, *God's Universe*, p. 49.

p. 52   *Dyson*: Quoted by John D. Barrow and Frank J. Tipler in *The Anthropic Cosmological Principle* (New York: Oxford University Press, 1986), p. 318.

Big Ideas and Biblical Wisdom

p. 54   *Big Ideas and Biblical Wisdom*: This section is adapted from David G. Myers, "Faith and Psychological Science," *Psychology and*

Christianity: Four Views, ed. Eric L. Johnson and Stanton Jones
(Downer's Grove, Ill.: InterVarsity Press, 2000).

p. 56   "*I am God* ...": Isaiah 46:9 (New Revised Standard Version).

p. 56   "*as the heavens* ...": Isaiah 55:9 (New Revised Standard Version).

p. 56   "*If we have understood* ...": Augustine's Sermon 52, ch. 6, sec. 16,
cited by Elizabeth Johnson, *She Who Is: The Mystery of God in Feminist
Theological Discourse* (New York: Crossroad, 1992), p. 105.

p. 60   "*Believe in God* ...": C. S. Lewis, *Mere Christianity* (New York:
Macmillan, 1960), bk. 3, ch. 9.

p. 61   *Princeton Seminary students:* John Darley and C. Daniel Batson,
"From Jerusalem to Jericho: A Study of Situational and
Dispositional Variables in Helping Behavior," *Journal of Personality
and Social Psychology*, 1973, *27*, 100–108.

Secularism and Civility

p. 65   *hard reality:* Phil Zuckerman, "Is Faith Good for Us?" *Free
Inquiry*, Aug.-Sept. 2006, pp. 35–38; Gregory S. Paul, "Cross-
National Correlations of Quantifiable Society Health with
Popular Religiosity and Secularism in the Prosperous
Democracy," *Journal of Religion and Society*, 2005, *7* [moses
.creighton.edu/JRS/2005/2005-11.html].

p. 65   *critique of secularism and civility analyses:* Gerson Moreno-Riaño,
Mark Caleb Smith, and Thomas Mach, "Religiosity, Secularism,
and Social Health: A Research Note," *Journal of Religion and Society*,
2006, *8* [moses.creighton.edu/JRS/2006/2006-1.html].

p. 66   *state divorce rates:* In three cases (California, Georgia, and
Hawaii), 2004 data were not available from *Statistical Abstract of
the United States, 2007*. For those I estimated the 2004 divorce
rate, assuming that the national drop in divorce rate from the
previously available date applied also to those states.

p. 69   *high school dropouts who smoke:* Jerald G. Backman and others,
*The Education-Drug Use Connection: How Successes and Failures in
School Relate to Adolescent Smoking, Drinking, Drug Use, and Delinquency*
(Philadelphia: Taylor & Francis, 2007).

p. 73   *religious engagement and marriage:* Mark A. Whisman and Douglas
K. Snyder, "Sexual Infidelity in a National Survey of American
Women: Differences in Prevalence and Correlates as a Function
of Method of Assessment," *Journal of Family Psychology*, 2007, *21*,

147–154; W. Bradford Wilcox, "Religion, Race, and Relationships in Urban America," Research Brief no. 5, Center for Marriage and Families, Institute for American Values, May 2007.

God and Gays

p. 74   *short book:* David G. Myers and Letha Dawson Scanzoni, *What God Has Joined Together: The Christian Case for Gay Marriage* (San Francisco: HarperOne, 2006).

p. 75   *earlier book:* David G. Myers, *The American Paradox: Spiritual Hunger in an Age of Plenty* (New Haven, Conn.: Yale University Press, 2000).

p. 78   *Jesus and the Pharisees:* Matthew 23:4 (Today's English Version).

p. 79   *church preoccupation:* Jonathan Haidt and Craig Joseph, "Intuitive Ethics: How Innately Prepared Intuitions Generate Culturally Variable Virtues," *Daedalus,* Fall 2004, pp. 55–66 [faculty.virginia .edu/haidtlab/articles/haidt.joseph.intuitive-ethics.pdf].

p. 81   *devil's advice:* C. S. Lewis, *The Screwtape Letters* (1942), in *The Complete C. S. Lewis Signature Classics* (San Francisco: HarperOne, 2007), p. 176.

(Nominal) Religion Feeds Prejudice

p. 82   "*Certainty . . .*": Sam Harris, *The End of Faith: Religion, Terror, and the Future of Reason* (New York: Norton, 2004), p. 13.

p. 83   "*Lord, Lord*": Matthew 7:21 (New Revised Standard Version).

p. 83   "*It makes prejudice . . .*": Gordon Allport, *The Nature of Prejudice* (Boston: Addison-Wesley, 1979), p. 444. (Originally published 1954.)

p. 85   "*The fruit of the Spirit . . .*": Galatians 5:22–23 (Revised Standard Version).

p. 86   "*Standing up . . .*": Martin Luther King Jr., "The Most Durable Power," sermon preached in Montgomery, Alabama, Nov. 6, 1956.

Godliness and Goodliness

p. 87   *Weinberg:* Quoted by George Johnson in "A Free-for-All on Science and Religion," *New York Times,* Nov. 21, 2006 [nytimes.com].

p. 88   *a martyr's death . . .*": Richard Dawkins, "Religion's Misguided Missiles," *Manchester Guardian*, Sept. 15, 2001 [guardian.co.uk].

p. 89   *most famous sermon:* Matthew 5:3–10 (New Revised Standard Version).

p. 91   *"If physical death . . .":* Martin Luther King Jr., "Saint Augustine, Florida," June 5, 1964.

p. 92   *positive psychology handbooks:* Christopher Peterson and Martin E. P. Seligman, *Character Strengths and Virtues: A Handbook and Classification* (New York: Oxford University Press, 2004); C. R. Snyder and Shane J. Lopez (eds.), *Handbook of Positive Psychology* (New York: Oxford University Press, 2002).

p. 92   *gratitude:* Robert Emmons and Charles Shelton, "Gratitude and the Science of Positive Psychology," in *Handbook of Positive Psychology.*

p. 93   *"Those who regularly attend . . .":* Peterson and Seligman, *Character Strengths and Virtues*, p. 562.

p. 93   *compassion:* Ibid., p. 326.

p. 93   *"Religions encourage people . . .":* Shalom Schwartz and Sipke Huismans, "Value Priorities and Religiosity in Four Western Religions," *Social Psychology Quarterly*, 1995, *58*, 88–107.

p. 94   *World War II chaplains:* This is my telling of the story from my *Social Psychology*, 9th ed. (New York: McGraw-Hill, 2008), pp. 456–457.

p. 95   *volunteering:* Peter L. Benson and others, "Intrapersonal Correlates of Nonspontaneous Helping Behavior," *Journal of Social Psychology*, 1980, 110, 87–95; David E. Hansen, Brian Vandenberg, and Miles L. Patterson, "The Effects of Religious Orientation on Spontaneous and Nonspontaneous Helping Behaviors," *Personality and Individual Differences*, 1995, 19, 101–104; Louis A. Penner, "Dispositional and Organizational Influences on Sustained Volunteerism: An Interactionist Perspective," *Journal of Social Issues*, 2002, 58, 447–467.

p. 96   *"highly spiritually committed":* George Gallup Jr., "Religion in America," *Gallup Report*, Mar. 1984.

p. 96   *religion rated:* Diane Colasanto, "Americans Show Commitment to Helping Those in Need," *Gallup Report*, Nov. 1989.

p. 96   *"responsibility to the poor":* Robert Wuthnow, *God and Mammon in America* (New York: Free Press, 1994).

p. 96   *civic involvement*: Robert Putnam, *Bowling Alone* (New York: Simon & Schuster, 2000), p. 67.

p. 97   *Gallup survey*: Virginia A. Hodgkinson, Murray S. Weitzman, and Arthur D. Kirsch, "From Commitment to Action: How Religious Involvement Affects Giving and Volunteering," in Robert Wuthnow, Virginia A. Hodgkinson, and Associates, *Faith and Philanthropy in America: Exploring the Role of Religion in America's Voluntary Sector* (San Francisco: Jossey-Bass, 1990).

p. 97   INDEPENDENT SECTOR *survey*: Ibid.; Virginia A. Hodgkinson and Murray S. Weitzman, *Giving and Volunteering in the United States* (Washington, D.C.: INDEPENDENT SECTOR, 1992).

p. 97   *"Religious people are more charitable . . .":* Center for Global Prosperity, *The Index of Global Philanthropy, 2007* (Washington, D.C.: Center for Global Prosperity, 2007), p. 22. Brooks is quoted here as well.

p. 97   *top philanthropists:* "America's Most Generous," *Fortune*, Jan. 13, 1997, p. 96.

p. 98   *seven largest charities:* Michael Guillen, *Can a Smart Person Believe in God?* (Nashville, Tenn.: Nelson, 2002), p. 87.

p. 98   *University of British Columbia researchers:* Azim F. Shariff and Ara Norenzayan, "God Is Watching You: Priming God Concepts Increases Prosocial Behavior in an Anonymous Economic Game," *Psychological Science*, 2007, 18, 803–809.

p. 98   *follow-up priming experiments:* Isabelle Pichon, Giulo Boccato, and Vassilis Saroglou, "Nonconscious Influences of Religion on Prosociality: A Priming Study," *European Journal of Social Psychology*, 2007, *37,* 1032–1045; Brandon Randolph-Seng and Michael E. Nielsen, "Honesty: One Effect of Primed Religious Representations," *International Journal for the Psychology of Religion*, 2007, 17, 303–315; Brandon Randolph-Seng and Michael E. Nielsen, "Is God Really Watching You? A Response to Shariff and Norenzayan," *International Journal for the Psychology of Religion*, forthcoming.

p. 98   *U.S. Values Survey:* Margaret Mooney Marini, "The Rise of Individualism in Advanced Industrial Societies," paper presented at annual meeting of the Population Association of America, Toronto, 1990.

p. 99   *delinquency studies:* Byron R. Johnson, Spencer De Li, David B. Larson, and Michael McCullough, "A Systematic Review of the Religiosity and Delinquency Literature: A Research Note," *Journal of Contemporary Criminal Justice*, 2000, 16, 32–52.

p. 99   twins study: Laura B. Koenig, Matt McGue, Robert F. Krueger, and
           Thomas J. Bouchard Jr., "Religiousness, Antisocial Behavior,
           and Altruism: Genetic and Environmental Mediation," *Journal of
           Personality*, 2007, 75, 265–290.

p. 99   pathogenic strains: Gordon Allport, "Behavioral Science, Religion,
           and Mental Health," *Journal of Religion and Health*, 1963, 2, 187–197.

p. 100   "vulgar caricatures": Terry Eagleton, "Lunging, Flailing,
           Mispunching" (review of Dawkins, *The God Delusion*), *London
           Review of Books*, Oct. 26, 2006.

p. 101   "men of deep religious faith": Walter Lippmann, *The Good Society*
           (New Brunswick, N.J.: Transaction, 2004), p. 382. (Originally
           published 1937.)

p. 102   Eric Liddell story: Sally Magnusson, *The Flying Scotsman* (London:
           Quartet Books, 1981); David J. Michell, "I Remember Eric
           Liddell," in *The Disciplines of the Christian Life*, ed. Eric Liddell
           (Nashville, Tenn.: Abingdon Press, 1985); Langdon Gilkey,
           Shantung Compound: The Story of Men and Women Under Pressure (New
           York: HarperCollins, 1966). Gilkey quotes are from p. 115.

p. 103   Shantung Compound liberation anniversary quotes: U.S. Embassy, Beijing,
           China, 2005 [beijing.usembassy-china.org.cn].

p. 105   closest comrade: A. P. Cullen, quoted in Magnusson, *Flying Scotsman*,
           pp. 175–176.

Happy Faith-Heads

p. 107   Hitchens, *God Is Not Great*, p. 16.

p. 107   *Gallup Organization, 1984*: George Gallup Jr., "Religion in
           America," *Gallup Report*, Mar. 1984.

p. 108   *Pew study*: "Are We Happy Yet?" *Pew Research Center*, Feb. 13, 2006
           [pewresearch.org].

p. 108   association to life satisfaction: Albert L. Winseman, "Congregational
           Engagement Index: Life Satisfaction and Giving," *Gallup Poll*, Feb.
           26, 2002 [poll.gallup.com].

p. 109   health and religiousness: Morris A. Okun and William A. Stock,
           "Correlates and Components of Subjective Well-Being Among
           the Elderly," *Journal of Applied Gerontology*, 1987, 6, 95–112.

p. 110   "the abolition of religion ...": Karl Marx, "Contribution to the
           Critique of Hegel's Philosophy of Right," quoted in Hitchens,
           God Is Not Great, p. 9.

p. 110   *religiously inactive new widows:* Carol D. Harvey, Gordon E. Barnes, and Leonard Greenwood, "Correlates of Morale Among Canadian Widowed Persons," *Social Psychiatry,* 1987, *22,* 65–72; Thomas H. McGloshen and Shirley L. O'Bryant, "The Psychological Well-Being of Older, Recent Widows," *Psychology of Women Quarterly,* 1988, *12,* 99–116; Judith M. Siegel and David H. Kuykendall, "Loss, Widowhood, and Psychological Distress Among the Elderly," *Journal of Consulting and Clinical Psychology,* 1990, *58,* 519–524.

p. 110   *mothers of developmentally challenged children:* W. N. Friedrich, D. S. Cohen, and L. T. Wilturner, "Specific Beliefs as Moderator Variables in Maternal Coping with Mental Retardation," *Children's Health Care,* 1988, *17,* 40–44.

p. 110   *people of faith:* Christopher G. Ellison, "Religious Involvement and Subjective Well-Being," *Journal of Health and Social Behavior,* 1991, *32,* 80–99; Daniel N. McIntosh, Roxane C. Silver, and Camille B. Wortman, "Religion's Role in Adjustment to a Negative Life Event: Coping with the Loss of a Child," *Journal of Personality and Social Psychology,* 1993, *65,* 812–821.

p. 110   *2003 statistical digest:* Timothy B. Smith, Michael E. McCullough, and Justin Poll, "Religiousness and Depression: Evidence for a Main Effect and the Moderating Influence of Stressful Life Events," *Psychological Bulletin,* 2003, *129,* 614–636.

p. 110   *Canadian follow-up study:* Marilyn Baetz, Rudy Bowen, Glenn Jones, and Tulay Koru-Sengul, "How Spiritual Values and Worship Attendance Relate to Psychiatric Disorders in the Canadian Population," *Canadian Journal of Psychiatry,* 2006, *51,* 654–661.

p. 111   *"rampant individualism":* Martin Seligman, "Boomer Blues," *Psychology Today,* Oct. 1988, pp. 50–55.

p. 111   *"We must delight in each other":* John Winthrop, "A Model of Christian Charity," in E. S. Morgan (ed.), *Puritan Political Ideas, 1558–1794* (Indianapolis: Bobbs-Merrill, 1965), p. 92.

p. 111   *Amish and depression:* J. A. Egeland and A. M. Hostetter, "Amish Study I: Affective Disorders Among the Amish, 1976–1980," *American Journal of Psychiatry,* 1983, *140,* 56–61; J. A. Egeland, A. M. Hostetter, and S. K. Eshleman, "Amish Study III: The Impact of Cultural Factors on Diagnosis of Bipolar Illness," *American Journal of Psychiatry,* 1983, *140,* 67–71.

p. 111   *correlation between religiousness and well-being:* Christopher G.
         Ellison, David A. Gay, and Thomas A. Glass, "Does Religious
         Commitment Contribute to Individual Life Satisfaction?" *Social
         Forces*, 1989, 68, 100–123.

p. 112   *Cyprian Norwid:* Quoted in Wladyslaw Tatarkiewicz, *Analysis of
         Happiness* (The Hague: Martinus Nijhoff, 1976).

p. 112   *loss of meaning and depression rate:* Seligman, "Boomer Blues."

p. 112   *National Longitudinal Survey of Freshmen:* Margarita Mooney, "Religion,
         College Grades, and Satisfaction Among Students at Elite Colleges
         and Universities," unpublished manuscript, Department of
         Sociology, University of North Carolina, 2008.

p. 112   *Viktor Frankl:* Victor Frankl, *Man's Search for Meaning: An Introduction to
         Logotherapy* (Boston: Beacon Press, 1962).

p. 113   *self-acceptance:* Paul Tillich, *Shaking the Foundations* (Gloucester,
         Mass.: Peter Smith, 1988).

p. 113   *Andrew Greeley:* Andrew Greeley, *Faithful Attraction* (New York: Tor
         Books, 1991).

p. 114   *significance of hope:* For more, see Jeff Greenberg, Mark Landau,
         Sheldon Solomon, and Tom Pyszczynski, "The Case for Terror
         Management as the Primary Function of Religion," manuscript
         submitted for publication.

p. 114   *"no evil and no good . . .":* Richard Dawkins, *River out of Eden: A
         Darwinian View of Life* (New York: Basic Books, 1995), p. 133.

p. 115   *belief in life after death:* Kevin J. Flannelly and others, "Belief in
         Life After Death and Mental Health: Findings from a National
         Survey," *Journal of Nervous and Mental Disease*, 2006, 194, 524–529.

p. 115   *"believers are more prosocial . . .":* David Sloan Wilson, "Beyond
         Demonic Memes: Why Richard Dawkins Is Wrong
         About Religion," *eSkeptic*, July 4, 2007 [skeptic.com/
         skeptic/07-07-04.html].

Healthy Faith-Heads

p. 116   *Healthy Faith-Heads:* This section is adapted from David G. Myers,
         "Religion and Human Flourishing," in *The Science of Subjective
         Well-Being*, ed. Randy Larsen and Michael Eid (New York:
         Guilford Press, 2008). Supporting citations appear there.

Does Explaining Religion Explain It Away?

p. 122   *survival of theology*: E. O. Wilson, *On Human Nature* (Cambridge, Mass.: Harvard University Press, 1978), p. 192.

p. 122   *religion as adaptive and beneficial*: David Sloan Wilson, *Darwin's Cathedral: Evolution, Religion, and the Nature of Society* (Chicago: University of Chicago Press, 2002).

p. 123   *seven deadly sins*: Dinesh D'Souza, *What's So Great About Christianity?* (Washington, D.C.: Regnery, 2007), p. 267.

p. 124   *scientific account of love*: Justin Barrett, quoted in Robin Marantz Henig, "Darwin's God," *New York Times*, Mar. 4, 2007 [nytimes .com].

p. 123   *explaining beliefs*: Keith Ward, *Is Religion Dangerous?* (Oxford: Lion Hudson, 2006), p. 174.

p. 124   *Archbishop Temple*: Quoted in M. A. Jeeves, *Psychology and Christianity: The View Both Ways* (Leicester, England: InterVarsity Press, 1976), p. 133.

p. 126   *"language of God"*: Francis Collins, *The Language of God: A Scientist Presents Evidence for Belief* (New York: Free Press, 2006).

p. 126   *Easterbrook on Dawkins*: Gregg Easterbrook, "Of Genes and Meaninglessness," *Science*, 1997, *277*, 892.

p. 127   *"motivated by the potent idea ..."*: Pointy Show Productions, program distributed at the preview showing of *Sold: Fighting the New Global Slave Trade*, London, Apr. 28, 2007.

The Leap of Faith

p. 128   Dawkins, *God Delusion*, p. 51.

p. 129   *"fanatical atheists"*: Albert Einstein, quoted in Walter Isaacson, "Einstein and Faith," *Time*, Apr. 5, 2007, pp. 44–48.

p. 130   *James quotes*: William James, *The Will to Believe and Other Essays in Popular Philosophy* (London: Longmans, Green, 1897), pp. 113, 120, 121.

Acknowledgments

I stand on the shoulders of more people than I can name, including countless fellow scholars for whom I feel a profound gratitude and whose work I have cited in my previous writings (some bits and pieces of which I have adapted in a few places in this volume). More immediately, I am indebted to the many friends who critiqued or encouraged earlier drafts of this little volume (but for which they bear no responsibility): Justin Barrett, James Brownson, Andrew Elliott, Julie Exline, Jonathan Haidt, Jaco Hamman, Ruth Hawley-Lowry, John Kotre, Donald Luidens, Alister McGrath, Carol Myers, Michael Nielsen, Judith Parr, Timothy Pennings, Anne Petersen, Marlin VanderWilt, Keith Ward, Charlotte Witvliet, and Everett Worthington.

Kathryn Brownson was, as always, a key supporter through her information gathering and editing.

This book would not exist were it not for my supportive agent, Susan Arellano, and my wonderfully

insightful and dedicated editor at Jossey-Bass, Sheryl
Fullerton.

Finally, I dedicate this book to my kindred-spirited
friend and professional colleague Malcolm Jeeves. What
Bono wrote when celebrating Al Gore as *Time* magazine's
2007 "Person of the Year" runner-up is also an apt
description of Malcolm: "His enduring and overarching
trait is . . . the pursuit of truth . . . scientific truth,
spiritual truth. That—and grace."

Although it is unlikely that any of these people
agree with this book's every word, they have collectively
guided me and encouraged this contribution to the
ongoing argument among friends.

D.G.M.

About the Author

David G. Myers is a social psychologist at Hope College in Holland, Michigan, and a communicator of psychological science to college students and the general public.

His scientific writings, supported by National Science Foundation fellowships and grants and recognized by the Gordon Allport Prize, have appeared in three dozen academic periodicals, including *Science, American Scientist,* and *Psychological Science*.

He has also written for four dozen magazines, from *Scientific American* to *Christian Century*. His seventeen books include texts for introductory and social psychology, works that relate psychological science to faith, and general audience books on happiness, intuition, sexual orientation, and hearing loss.

Myers is a Seattle native, an all-weather bicyclist, and a national advocate of hearing-aid-compatible assistive listening (see hearingloop.org). David and Carol Myers are the parents of three adult children.